An Introduc

Edinburgh Textbooks on the English Language

General Editor
Heinz Giegerich, Professor of English Linguistics, University of Edinburgh

Editorial Board
Laurie Bauer (University of Wellington)
Derek Britton (University of Edinburgh)
Olga Fischer (University of Amsterdam)
Rochelle Lieber (University of New Hampshire)
Norman Macleod (University of Edinburgh)
Donka Minkova (UCLA)
Edgar W. Schneider (University of Regensburg)
Katie Wales (University of Leeds)
Anthony Warner (University of York)

TITLES IN THE SERIES INCLUDE

An Introduction to English Sociolinguistics

Graeme Trousdale

Edinburgh University Press

© Graeme Trousdale, 2010

Edinburgh University Press Ltd
22 George Square, Edinburgh

www.euppublishing.com

Typeset in 10.5/12 Janson
by Servis Filmsetting Ltd, Stockport, Cheshire, and
printed and bound in Great Britain by
CPI Antony Rowe, Chippenham and Eastbourne

A CIP record for this book is available from the British Library

ISBN 978 0 7486 2324 2 (hardback)
ISBN 978 0 7486 2325 9 (paperback)

Contents

Figures and tables

Figures

Tables

Acknowledgements

I would like to thank Lynn Clark, Heinz Giegerich, Richard Hudson, Paul Kerswill, Remco Knooihuizen, Miriam Meyerhoff, Emma Moore and Joan Swann for very helpful comments on an earlier, draft version of this book. I would also like to thank both Sarah Edwards and Esmé Watson at Edinburgh University Press for their unwavering support and advice.

I am grateful to various publishers for permission to use copyright material in the following figures:

a the University of Leeds for Figure 4.1 (taken from Orton, Harold, Stewart Sanderson and John Widdowson. 1978. *The Linguistic Atlas of England*. Leeds: University of Leeds)

b Wiley-Blackwell for: Figure 4.2 (taken from Trudgill, Peter. 1999. *The Dialects of England*. 2nd edition. Oxford: Blackwell, p. 34); Figure 5.1 (taken from Chambers, J. K. 2002. Patterns of variation including change. In J. K. Chambers, Peter Trudgill and Natalie Schilling-Estes (eds), *The Handbook of Language Variation and Change*. Oxford: Blackwell, p. 360); and Figure 8.2 (based on data from Stuart-Smith, Jane and Claire Timmins. 2007. Talkin' Jockney: Accent change in Glaswegian. *Journal of Sociolinguistics* 11, p. 236)

c Cambridge University Press for Figure 5.2 (taken from Eckert, Penelope. 1988. Adolescent social structure and the spread of linguistic change. *Language in Society* 17, p. 200)

d Andre Deutsch for Figure 4.3 (based on data from Petyt, K. M. 1980. *The Study of Dialect: An Introduction to Dialectology*. London: Deutsch, p. 189).

To readers

This is a book about varieties of the English language, both now and in the past, and about the way in which the diversity that characterises such varieties comes to be used by individuals and communities of speakers in order to achieve interpersonal, social and political goals. In other words, it is about both the linguistic form of varieties of English, and the function of those varieties in communities across the world. In order to understand why varieties of English have the form and function that they do, we will make use of general research into the relationship between language and society, a discipline known as 'sociolinguistics'. Sociolinguistics covers a wide range of intellectual inquiry, and this book will not cover all aspects of the sociolinguistic enterprise. For example, this book does not deal in any depth with the range of methodologies used to investigate sociolinguistic variation in English (see Tagliamonte 2006 for an introduction to sociolinguistic method); nor does it deal in depth with aspects of discourse structure, conversational analysis, sexism and language, and many other topics which you might expect to find in an introductory book on general sociolinguistics. What this book does is draw on selected aspects of the findings of sociolinguistic research in order to illustrate a range of interesting things about the English language.

The first part of the book is concerned primarily with the function of English in various societies (though as we will see throughout the book, it is often difficult to discuss the function of English without making some reference to aspects of linguistic form). The first chapter is concerned with English as a linguistic and as a social concept. In this chapter, we will consider what many people might consider a surprising question: is English a language? In order to answer that question, we will need to establish what is meant by both 'English' and 'language', and we will see that when we use linguistic criteria (for example, sounds, words or sentences) to try to establish what 'English' is, in order to distinguish it from other languages such as 'French', 'Navajo' or 'Scots', some very interesting and problematic issues arise. When we use social, cultural or geographic criteria (for example, that there is a correct variety of English, or that English can be defined by its use in specific domains, or that English is the language spoken in particular places such as England and Australia) to try to establish what 'English' is, we run into other, equally interesting, and equally problematic issues. The second chapter looks at communities and individuals who speak English. In this chapter, we look at three different things: the notion of a speech community; a global network of English speakers; and the relationship between the individual and the English language. The third chapter of this book considers English explicitly as a sociopolitical concept, where we look at the place of English in (often government-authorised) language planning, and domains of English use in multilingual communities.

The second part of the book looks more closely at formal character-istics of varieties of English. Chapter 4 begins by locating the study of social variation in English within a larger context of dialectology (the study of varieties of language, usually regional varieties). We will also consider some of the ways in which English varies depending on the social characteristics of the speaker, the social context in which the discourse takes place, and the nature of the speaker's audience. The intersection of dialectology and sociolinguistics in terms of the social dimensions of geographic space is also discussed. Chapter 5 is con-cerned with the relationship between social variation in present-day English and the study of ongoing change in the language. We examine some of the insights that variationist sociolinguistics has provided for the study of language change in general, and change in varieties of English in particular. In this chapter, we will also consider the impor-tant issue of language maintenance – given the power associated with Standard English, which has grown since the beginnings of the standard variety about five hundred years ago, why do non-standard, vernacular varieties of English continue to thrive? Chapter 6 continues the theme of language variation and change by looking at sociolinguistics and the history of English. In this chapter we cover topics from all periods of the history of English, from whether we can sensibly talk about social variation in the earliest recorded forms of English in the Anglo-Saxon period, through to the sociolinguistics of polite and refined English usage in the nineteenth century, and the future of English.

Chapters 7 and 8 are about contact, and the linguistic consequences of contact between speakers of different varieties. These varieties might be different languages, or they might be dialects of English – what we see is that the linguistic processes involved in both cases are very similar. Chapter 7 looks at English in contact with other languages, picking up some of the themes from Chapter 3, but concentrating on the formal properties of English in such contact scenarios, where language changes as a result of normal interaction between speakers, rather than authorised intervention. What linguistic properties or characteristics are found in varieties which have emerged from short-term and long-term contact between speakers of English and speakers of other languages? Chapter 8 looks at dialect contact, examining the kinds of varieties that emerge both through long-term contact at boundaries between dialect areas of English, and also as a result of mass migration to newly created communities. These communities may have been established fairly recently (as in the case of new towns in the United Kingdom) or much longer ago (as in the case of migrations to New Zealand).

The ninth chapter is concerned with the place of sociolinguistics within a larger theory of the structure of English, and of language more generally. We will consider the interplay of linguistic and social constraints on variation, and then outline some of the ways in which some theories have attempted to incorporate sociolinguistic findings into their framework for language structure, as well as considering the justification for such an incorporation. How do we bring together the important findings from quantitative sociolinguistics and the equally important findings from theoretical linguistics? This is a challenging and exciting aspect of research into why language varies in the way that it does, and how we should model such variation. The final part of the book is a concluding chapter which tries to bring together some of the themes in the rest of the book.

In what follows, I assume minimal knowledge of formal aspects of linguistic description, discussing particular linguistic features as they emerge. Specific linguistic terms are defined on first use. An appendix has been provided which gives some guidance on phonetic transcription conventions.

All of the chapters conclude with some questions for discussion. Some of these questions are designed for more general discussion; others are designed to check your understanding of some of the concepts introduced in the chapter. But more generally I hope that this book encourages you to think of your own questions about English sociolinguistics, and how you might think of a project which could answer those questions.

Further reading

Each chapter of this book concludes with some reading on the specific topics introduced therein. Here I make some suggestions for general reading on sociolinguistics which complement this book. These texts include data from languages other than English, and are also typically about sociolinguistic theory and practice more generally.

An excellent introduction to many aspects of sociolinguistics is Meyerhoff (2006). Other very comprehensive introductions include Holmes (2001), Mesthrie et al. (2009) and Wardhaugh (2010); Chambers (2003) presents a particularly clear account of modern sociolinguistic theory. For handbooks, which present summaries of the main research grouped around particular topics, Chambers et al. (2002) is the standard for language variation and change, while Coulmas (1998) explores sociolinguistics more generally. In terms of a general theory of cognition, language and society, the textbook which comes closest to this one is Hudson (1996), though that book is not concerned with English exclusively. For introductions to sociolinguistic methodology, including the quantitative analysis of variable data, see Milroy and Gordon (2003) and (as mentioned above), Tagliamonte (2006). A comprehensive explanation of sociolinguistic terms is provided by Trudgill (2003) and Swann et al. (2004).

1 What is 'English'?

1.1 Overview

Most of you reading this book will have a fairly good idea of what English is, and what it represents, and this is true no matter where in the world you come from. One of the reasons for this is associated with the world-wide spread of English, and the status that English has as a global language. English is associated by many with power and prestige: it is seen as the language of electronic media, the language of business, the language people often turn to when other means of communication fail – English is the world's *lingua franca* or common language. It fulfils a global function which other languages do not. There may be more speakers of Mandarin Chinese than there are of English, but Mandarin does not have the same kind of influence in the same number of countries as English does. The number of speakers of Spanish as either a first or second language might be growing rapidly on the American continent, but this does not match the total number of speakers learning English as a second language, in countries as diverse as Germany and Namibia. The spread of English, from its Germanic origins in the fifth century CE to its status as the only linguistic superpower of the twenty-first century, is not simply a fascinating subject of intellectual inquiry; it has also meant that English has become the language in which much international intellectual inquiry is reported, in research papers at conferences or research articles in journals, irrespective of the topic.

But this global spread has not been cost-free. As English has forced its way into a number of different communities across the world, local languages – and with them, the culture that those languages embody – have died out. 'Killer English' is often thought of as a recent phenomenon: it has been linked to the rise of mass communication, and to the political and economic might of two countries, the United States and the United Kingdom, from the nineteenth century onwards. However, even at its inception, English has been linked with the displacement

1

and marginalisation of indigenous languages: in the British Isles, after the arrival of the Germanic tribes in the mid-fifth century, the Celtic languages (such as Welsh, Cornish and Gaelic) were pushed further and further north and/or west: some have fared better than others, in terms of the number of existing native speakers.

Such accounts – of English as an emancipating language, or of English as a language of destruction – are often presented as if English somehow had a life of its own, distinct from the practices of those individuals who speak and write English on a daily basis. And this of course cannot be the case. There might well be a correlation between the spread of English and certain patterns of cultural and socioeconomic changes; but this is correlation, not causation. So it is important to keep quite distinct the speakers of a language and the language itself. And it is equally important to establish the relationship between the forms of English and the function of the language in different communities. Thus one of the aims of this book is to explore the relationship between formal characteristics of the English language – its sounds, spellings and grammar, for instance – and the speakers and writers who make use of English to fulfil a set of specific functions (which may or may not be highly specialised to the group in question). English, like any other language, must be considered as part of the social practices of the groups of speakers and writers who use it for particular communicative purposes. The purpose of this chapter is to investigate what this 'English' might be, and how and why it is used in the ways in which it is used in a range of different communities.

Here are some examples of texts (some spoken, some written) which might be counted as instances of English. The first is an extract from Shakespeare's *Hamlet*, written around 1600; the second is a transcription of part of a conversation between a linguist and a young man from the United Kingdom; the third is from an American Express credit card statement; the fourth is from a blog (and there is enough evidence there to suggest that the writer comes from the north-east of England); the fifth is from Faulkner's *The Sound and the Fury*, published in 1929; the sixth is from a track ('In Life') by a Nigerian hip-hop group called the Plantashun Boiz.

(1)   To be, or not to be; that is the question:
         Whether 'tis nobler in the mind to suffer
         The slings and arrows of outrageous fortune,
         Or to take arms against a sea of troubles
         And by opposing, end them. (Shakespeare, *Hamlet*, III, i, 57–61)
(2)   yeah well . when we've done our GCSEs and everything . umm I

don't know we'll maybe make a tape or something when we've got some better songs . and . well we'll just send it off to NME and stuff but also our uncle knows a man who's . I think he's coming to the one on Tuesday and they'll like . you know apparently we're playing in this . charity one in June or something at . Hunter Hospital or something and there's a band that played there last year called . oh I don't know er but they got a record deal from that concert (Cheshire 2007: 156, emphases removed; the full stops here indicate brief pauses in speech)

(3) If you do not pay the full amount outstanding we will allocate your payment to the outstanding balance in a specific order which is set out in the summary box contained in this statement. The way in which payments are allocated can make a significant difference to the amount of interest you will pay until the balance is cleared completely.

(4) Whats the lamest Most patheticest (<< dunno if thats a word) excsue [*sic*] youve ever heard?
ive heard a few bad ones like haha
the mother was singin the wrong words to a song the neet and i was geet
"ur singin it rong mam" and she went "ii ana i was just testin to see what it soudns [*sic*] like wiv them words in" (http://www.northern-rave.co.uk/viewtopic.php?f=55&t=14293; accessed 28 June 2009)

(5) "Dont talk to me about no show. Time I get done over this here tub I be too tired to lift my hand to do nothing."
"I bet you be there." Luster said. "I bet you was there last night. I bet you all be right there when that tent open." (William Faulkner, *The Sound and the Fury* New York: Vintage, 1990 p. 15)

(6) Omoge show me right from wrong   [Baby]
Jowo wa sinu aiye mi   [Please come into my life]
Ko je kin da bi okunrin   [Let me be like a man]
We'll be loving one on one
Till we see the morning sun
(Pidgin rap)
Ah ah ah,
Ah check am
Baby anytime I see your face
My heart go start to scatter
After I check am na you be my desire
I no dey tell you dis because I wan dey talk am
I dey tell you dis based on say na so I dey mean am (Omoniyi 2006: 199; emphases removed; translations of Yoruba in square brackets)

These extracts are intended simply to give some idea about the kind of data, which appear in a range of texts, which might be referred to as English (though note that whether we should classify them all as instances of 'English' is a matter of debate). First, we have to consider whether we are justified in talking about 'the English language', as if it were some sort of unified, identifiable whole. This may strike you as something of a non-issue, because the concept of 'the English language' is so well entrenched in our minds. But we will see that the existence of a 'language' as an object of linguistic inquiry (as opposed to a cultural belief shared by members of a community) has been the subject of some debate within linguistics as a whole, and within the discipline of socio-linguistics in particular.

1.2 Languages and dialects

We need to begin by examining what is meant by the terms 'language' and 'dialect', both for the linguist, and for the typical language user. That such terms have both popular and scientific meanings (which can lead to uncertainty and confusion when the terms are applied to real-life situations) has been recognised for some time (Haugen 1966). But even within the discipline of linguistic inquiry, the terms are not always used with the same meanings – for instance, both 'dialect' and 'language' have been associated with nationhood and identity in sociolinguistic literature, but such issues are not usually of interest to linguists working on matters pertaining to the language faculty (that part of human cognitive ability which is considered by some linguists to be unique to language, different from other parts of cognition) and structural patterns and constraints in human language (though these linguists will still use the terms 'language' and 'dialect' when discussing data of various kinds). Many theoretical linguists are interested in what we might call Language (the language faculty), which is manifested in various languages across the globe. Our concern here is with those manifestations (that is, languages, not Language), but we will return to the issue of the language faculty in the final chapter.

A dictionary definition of the terms 'language' and 'dialect' is a useful place to start, because dictionaries typically provide definitions on which at least some people in the community agree. One function of a dictionary is to represent what most speakers of a given variety will accept as an accurate meaning of any given concept: note that this is true both of dictionaries of the standard language in various countries (for example, the *Oxford English Dictionary* in the United Kingdom, or *Webster's Third New International Dictionary* in the United States), and of dictionaries of local varieties (dialect dictionaries such as the *Dictionary of Smoky Mountain English* in the United States, Montgomery and Hall 2004). The online version of the *Oxford English Dictionary* (www.oed. com) has the following definitions[1] of 'language' and 'dialect':

> Language: The system of spoken or written communication used by a particular country, people, community, etc., typically consisting of words used within a regular grammatical and syntactic structure.
>
> Dialect: 1. Manner of speaking, language, speech; esp. a manner of speech peculiar to, or characteristic of, a particular person or class; phraseology, idiom. 2.a. One of the subordinate forms or varieties of a language arising from local peculiarities of vocabulary, pronunciation, and idiom. (In relation to modern languages usually spec[ifically]: A variety of speech differing from the standard or literary 'language'; a provincial method of speech, as in 'speakers of dialect'.) Also in a wider sense applied to a particular language in its relation to the family of languages to which it belongs.

Notice that such definitions illustrate how hard it can be to distinguish a language from a dialect: the last part of the definition of *dialect* suggests that one meaning of *dialect* is 'language'! But these definitions provide a useful starting point to allow us to explore what we mean by 'the English language' and 'dialects of English'.

First, note how the definitions explicitly link linguistic concepts (for example, "The system of spoken or written communication ... typically consisting of words used within a regular grammatical and syntactic structure") with social concepts (for example, "used by a particular country, people, community, etc."). We therefore need to consider what kind of criteria we should use to identify varieties as 'languages' or 'dialects': linguistic, social, or both. Second, part of the definition of 'dialect' suggests that a dialect is in a subordinate position relative to a language. That subordination is both spatial and social: a dialect is smaller than a language (being restricted to a particular local or geographical area) and it carries less prestige (being different from the standard language). Third, there is a suggestion that 'dialect' can be used to describe the language of an individual. The more common term for the language of an individual is 'idiolect'. However, it is clear that we will need to consider how the linguistic characteristics of the individual are related to larger concepts such as language and dialect. Note also that the social concepts used (for example, 'people' and 'community') are really rather generalised, and as such might refer to a group of people which extends beyond a country (for example, people who speak English as a second or other language in the European Union might be said to speak 'Euro English'), or to a group that defines itself (or is defined by others) by a shared ethnic heritage (for example, speakers who make use of African American English), or to a group that inhabits only part of a nation (for example, the English of residents of Sydney, Australia).

1.3 Linguistic and social criteria for different languages

Given that one part of our dictionary definitions suggests that a dialect can be a language, we need to consider quite carefully how we can separate out the two, to come to a better understanding of what differentiates dialects of English from the English language. One criterion often invoked in attempts to distinguish between languages and dialects is that of mutual intelligibility: if speaker A is intelligible to speaker B, no matter how great the linguistic differences might be, then they are speaking the same language (although they may be speaking different dialects of the same language); by contrast, if speaker A is not intelligible to speaker B, then they are speaking different languages. Unfortunately, as Hudson (1996) observes, this does not really tell us anything about languages: it tells us something only about speakers A and B, so the intelligibility criterion is a property of individual speakers, not of languages or dialects. Essentially, the idiolects of speakers A and B have sufficient overlap to enable successful communication between A and B. Furthermore, there are the well-known examples (which appear in practically every textbook on sociolinguistics, and this book is no exception) of mutually intelligible 'languages' (like Swedish and Norwegian) and of mutually unintelligible (spoken) 'dialects' (like Mandarin and Cantonese). A particularly good example of the problem of the mutual intelligibility criterion is Scots and its relationship to English. It is the case that some speakers of Scots are not fully intelligible – even if they speak slowly – to some speakers of English. This illustrates the point made by Haugen (1966: 926), who wrote that "[b]etween total incomprehension and total comprehension there is a large twilight zone of partial comprehension in which something occurs that we may call 'semicommunication'".

The mutual intelligibility criterion reinforces the widespread belief that languages can be defined on linguistic grounds. Jones (2002: 2), using the examples of Swahili and Navajo, has suggested that the linguistic differences – at the phonological, lexical and syntactic levels – are so great that they have to be considered as different languages. He then goes on, however, to point out that other linguistic varieties such as Provençal and Catalan have been classified as languages on sociopolitical grounds. A further example of such a process concerns the development of Serbian, Croatian and Bosnian as languages following the Balkan conflict in the 1990s (Crystal 2000: 9) – these languages are formally very similar, but the social changes have been very significant. These two ways of identifying varieties as languages are related to the 'Abstand' and 'Ausbau' distinctions made by Kloss (1967). Abstand – or 'language by distance' – is concerned with formal distinctions, while Ausbau – 'language by development' – is concerned with functional distinctions. Abstand languages are those which are distinct because of their formal linguistic development; Ausbau languages are those which are distinct because of their functional sociolinguistic development. Using the examples mentioned above, we would say that Swahili and Navajo are Abstand languages, while Serbian, Croatian and Bosnian are Ausbau languages. One potential problem with such approaches (that is, those which consider both linguistic and sociopolitical criteria for establishing which varieties constitute a language) is that they use two very different sets of rules for classifying the same group of objects, so in some cases you end up with 'linguistic languages' and in other cases 'social languages'.

How does this relate specifically to English? Consider the following language varieties: 'German', 'English', 'Scots' and 'American'. Which of these are languages? Most people are of the opinion that German and English are definitely languages, American definitely is not, and Scots is hard to classify. Note that there is no direct correlation between language and nation (otherwise both Scots and American would be considered as languages); nor can we appeal exclusively to formal features, since the grammars of English, Scots and American are much more similar to each other than any of them are to German. They are all clearly related to each other historically, but the formal and functional divergence of German from the other varieties is sufficiently great that there is widespread agreement that this is a different language. At various points in history, both Scots and American have officially been classified in different communities as languages. For instance, the European Charter for Regional or Minority Languages, ratified by the United Kingdom in 2001, specified that Scots, in both Scotland and Northern Ireland, should be seen as a minority language, and afforded both protection and promotion; and an act of legislature in Illinois in 1923 proclaimed that "the official language of the state of Illinois shall be known hereafter as the American language and not as the English language" (Act of Legislature of Illinois, chapter 127, section 178, 1923 – cited in McArthur 1998: 221).

Such political intervention in the classification and organisation of linguistic varieties is known as language planning, which we will address in Chapter 3, by considering the formal and functional issues involved. Because there is little consensus on the formal and functional differences between Scots and English, some people erroneously consider Scots to be simply 'bad English'. However, this concept of 'good' and 'bad' varieties is another factor we need to take into consideration when we think about the classification of different varieties into languages and dialects.

1.4 Good and bad English

An alternative way of thinking about what 'English' is is to ask speakers of the language, and evaluate their attitude towards English. This can result in quite a different understanding of the concept: research has shown that speakers often don't think about languages and dialects in their 'dictionary' senses, preferring instead to categorise varieties of English as either 'good' or 'bad' (Preston 2002). This way of thinking about varieties applies equally to spoken and written forms of English. When we consider such language attitudes, we are exploring in part folk beliefs, not simply about varieties of language, but also about speakers of those varieties. In other words, we are exploring something about language ideology.

It is often this issue that receives the most attention in the popular press, and in non-academic books about variation and change in English. Consider, for example, the following from a recent book on aspects of English style by the BBC radio and television presenter John Humphrys:

> (7) I don't like glottal stops (especially when they are adopted by public-school-educated politicians because they think it makes them sound cool) and I don't like people saying 'fink' unless they have a speech impediment. (Humphrys 2004: 228)

The writer here mentions two widespread changes affecting current British English: T-Glottaling (the pronunciation of the intervocalic consonant in words like *butter* as [ʔ],[2] so *butter* is pronounced [bʌʔə]) and TH-Fronting (the pronunciation of the initial consonant in words like *think* as [f], so *think* is pronounced [fɪŋk]). The justification for the writer's dislike of the glottal stop has less to do with the sound itself than with a particular set of speakers who use it for a particular function. This association of speech with speaker type is expressed overtly by the following child from Widnes, in the north-west of England:

(8) I dislike London accent because they are stuck up snobs. (Cheshire and Edwards 1993: 42)

Such views are by no means uncommon, nor are they restricted to contemporary British English varieties. The following comes from an article in the *New York Times* of Sunday 11 February 1906 (p. 10), which reports a meeting of New York teachers, where anxieties about the influence of immigrants (among other things) on the standards of literacy among graduating seniors were expressed by Mr Mitchill, Head of the Boys' High School, Brooklyn:

(9) In our peculiar population comparatively few of the pupils live in homes where good English is spoken, and when they are gathered in large classes the personal influence of the teacher can hardly be felt. Just listen to pupils from our public schools when they are on the streets, unless they happen to live in homes where good English is spoken. They will talk among themselves in the same slovenly lingo that the ordinary street boy uses.

As Edwards (1982: 20) writes, "people's reactions to language varieties reveal much of their perception of the speakers of these varieties", and one of the reasons that such research on language attitudes is so important is because it helps us to understand some of the relationships between language and identity that we will explore in later chapters. But also, such work in perceptual dialectology – where varieties are distinguished on the basis of the attitudes and beliefs held by individuals and groups – enables us to think about another way of identifying varieties of English. It is important to note that there may be a mismatch between attitudes held by people about varieties of English and data collected by linguists in the field (for example, there is no evidence that people from Newcastle in England talk any more slowly than other speakers of English), but sometimes the correlations between perceived boundaries between different accents and dialects, and the boundaries established by regional dialectologists, are quite strong (Niedzielski and Preston 2003).

Associated with this notion of good and bad forms of English is the doctrine of correctness: some speakers will often report that a particular way of saying something is just plain wrong. Such 'errors' have included grammatical features like multiple negation (for example, *I ain't never been there*), and the use of 'redundant' words (for example, *added* in *added bonus*). In many cases, the features that are reported as wrong either used to be fairly common in the earlier history of the language but failed to make it into the 'standard language' (see Section 1.6 below) when it was codified, or are currently undergoing change. This change may be incipient only in a very specific domain, and even in a restricted set of constructions. For example, in discourse about sports, the word *result* sometimes does not simply mean 'outcome', but has ameliorated to mean 'positive outcome', which explains why *we came away with a result* is not as nonsensical as it might first appear to be. Some features are more widely condemned than others, and these features become less frequently discussed the more widely they are used by speakers of the standard variety. For example, multiple negation is still highly salient as a non-standard feature; by contrast, fewer people would consider the placement of *only* in example (10) as worthy of comment:

(10)   The thieves broke into our kitchen but they only took the toaster.

Some of the (self-appointed) guardians of English usage might complain that *only* here modifies the verb *took* (that is, the only thing the thieves did was take the toaster – they didn't clean it or rewire it), and the 'correct' version would be:

(11)   The thieves broke into our kitchen but they took only the toaster.

But this is not as widely condemned as many other errors, because examples like (10) are fairly common in the speech of Standard English users. We will look again at the issue of correct usage in Chapter 6, when we look at some aspects of the history of English.

1.5 The native speaker of English

Just as we have seen that there are common-sense, folk-linguistic views of linguistic varieties, so there are common-sense views of speakers of those varieties. One such view is that of a native speaker, a concept as problematic as that of a language. The notion of a native speaker is an issue relevant to all languages, but perhaps especially to English, given the fact that there are more speakers of English as a second or other language than speakers of English as a first or native language (Crystal 2003: 68). What precisely does it mean to be a native speaker of a language? The common-sense view is that a native speaker of English is one who is born in a community of other speakers of English, and acquires his language from them (primarily from his parents or caregivers). Particularly, a native speaker may be someone to whom others may turn for guidance as to what is acceptable and what is not in the language in question: a native speaker of English might be asked by non-native speakers whether a particular definition of a word is correct, or whether a particular grammatical construction is better or worse than another, though this very much depends on the social context, and the nature of the community in question. Thus the 'arbitration' role of the native speaker is problematised when one considers communities (such as some of those in India) in which non-native speakers use English for such a wide variety of purposes that the views of the native speaker become less and less relevant, and more local norms of usage emerge.

One aspect of being a native speaker is indeed a sense of community, and with that, a sense of identity. Being a native speaker of English gives you a different identity from the group of individuals who are native speakers of French: it's a way of establishing who is part of the group, and who isn't. The interesting issue here concerns bilinguals: are those individuals from Montreal in Canada who are bilingual speakers of French and English, for example, members of both groups simultaneously, do they switch from one group to the other when they code-switch between French and English, or do they belong to neither group, forming instead a group of their own? We will return to this issue in the following chapter, when we explore the notion of community in more detail. Such acts of identity (Le Page and Tabouret-Keller 1985) are relevant too at the more local level of dialect. Some speakers align themselves with what they perceive as a particular local variety. Within England, for example, this might be as a 'northerner', or more locally as a 'north-westerner', a 'Mancunian' (someone from Manchester), and so on, down to the negotiation and marking of identity at a very small group level (see further Chapters 2 and 4).

As noted above, the input to acquisition is typically the language of the parents or caregivers, a very specific social group. In English-speaking communities, when the child goes to school, he or she will be expected to acquire another variety, which may differ significantly in form, and will certainly differ in function, from the variety spoken at home: Standard English.

1.6 Standard English

The concept of a standard language is a critical one in sociolinguistics. The creation of a standard variety of any language is very much a sociopolitical one (Milroy and Milroy 1998), as part of the language policy of a particular community. In other words, the standard language of a community will fulfil a particular set of functions: for example, it will often be the variety used in the broadcast and print media, in education and in government. Furthermore, by and large, members of a community agree on what counts as Standard English, so there is an agreed set of forms which make up the standard variety. For example, although multiple negation, as illustrated by (12), is very common in non-standard speech and writing, it does not feature in written and spoken Standard English.

(12) He ain't never done nothing.

None the less, it is the case that Standard English varies. Sometimes, just as is the case with non-standard English, the variation is overt, noted, and commented on (such that people will criticise those who say *between you and I*, rather than *between you and me*, or *it's entirely up to yourself*, rather than *it's entirely up to you*). People who use these variants are undoubtedly speakers of Standard English, using any other criteria; so despite occasional criticism of such forms by purists, they have come to form part of the standard variety.

How precisely does Standard English vary? First we can distinguish between written Standard English and spoken Standard English. Some things are peculiar to just written language (for example, spelling variants, such as *colour/color*) or just spoken language (for example, pronunciation variants, such as the alternative ways of pronouncing the first syllable of *transmission*). Grammatical variation occurs in both spoken and written Standard English. Some examples of variation in standard grammar which could be written or spoken include:

(13) I've not written to him vs. I haven't written to him.
(14) I dreamed of you last night vs. I dreamt of you last night.
(15) May I be excused? vs. Can I be excused?

Some of these features may be undergoing change (for example, the regularisation of past tense marking on verbs means that irregular forms like *dream – dreamt* are shifting into a different category), while others may denote differing regional standards (for example, in (13), contraction of the auxiliary verb and subject (that is, *I've*) in negative sentences is more common in the northern part of England, while contraction of the auxiliary verb and the negative marker (that is, *haven't*) is more common in the south.)

This leads us to the second way in which Standard English varies. Different communities have different Standard Englishes. There is a Standard American English and a Standard British English, for instance. These two are probably the best-known of all Standard Englishes, because they are the ones that are typically used as models for teaching English as a second or other language. These two standards vary in a number of ways: in terms of pronunciation (for example, whether the /r/ is pronounced in *card*), grammar (for example, whether the past participle of *get* is *got* or *gotten*), vocabulary (for example, whether the storage compartment at the rear of a car is called a *boot* or a *trunk*) and spelling (for example, *center* vs. *centre*). Other standards are emerging too, however – in India, in Singapore, and in a number of African countries, for instance. We will discuss the sociolinguistics of these varieties in later chapters (Chapters 3 and 7); here we can simply note the paradox of English as a global language: the more English is used as a common, shared, global language, the more fragmented it becomes.

The third way in which Standard English varies is in terms of formality. In both written and spoken Standard English, speakers may use different linguistic forms and patterns to mark a more careful style. For instance, formal, written, Standard English prose tends to have a greater incidence of Latinate vocabulary (for example, *incidence*, *Latinate* and *vocabulary!*) than informal writing. Similarly, there may be a higher frequency of particular grammatical forms, like the subjunctive – to mark hypotheticality, as in (16), or the laying down of an obligation, as in (17) – in formal Standard English:

(16) If he were here, we could go. (cf. If he was here, we could go.)
(17) I insist she be given more time to finish her essay. (cf. I insist she is given more time to finish her essay.)

Finally, there is the issue of reactions to standardisation. The standard language is disseminated in a community usually via the media and (more importantly) the school. And when we look at the development of Standard English in the history of the language (see Chapter 6) we notice that standardisation has been more successful in terms of spelling than in any other area of language (grammar, pronunciation, and so on). Spelling variation used to be very common in English, such that well-educated individuals of high social status would use different spellings from one another, and indeed display a high incidence of intra-writer variation; but the advent of standardisation reduced spelling variation to a minimum. However, with the development of electronic communication systems, there has been a significant change in the way in which English is written. Instant messaging over the internet, and text messaging via mobile/cell phones, have created a new set of spellings that have been conventionalised to differing degrees. It is probably too early to speak of a standard text language, but clearly there are conventions, and these conventions manifest themselves differently in different communities, although similar practices may be adopted (for example, the French text for *l8r* 'later' is *A+* 'à plus (tard)' = 'later').

1.7 Summary

Blommaert (2005) discusses some of the ways in which 'English' is used in discourse about language. He suggests that 'English' and other language names are part of "folk ideologies of language" (Blommaert 2005: 390). It is clear that 'English' does have a meaning for speakers, even if it does not correspond precisely to a set of linguistic phenomena, so a dictionary of English will never be able to list all the words used by speakers who claim to speak 'English', and a grammar of English will never be able to list all the constructions. There can be little doubt that the concept of 'the English language' is well entrenched in many people's minds. In the rest of this book, we explore some of the forms and functions of different kinds of Englishes; but right from the outset, it is important to question the existence of a set of linguistic forms that are shared by a group of people that go together to constitute 'English'. In this chapter, we have explored the concepts of 'language' and 'dialect' in relation to English, and shown that such terms might best be considered as social phenomena, rather than terms which we can use to describe a speaker's mental knowledge of language. We have shown that it is important to distinguish between spoken and written language, because they are structured differently, and are subject to different degrees and kinds of standardisation and codification. Particularly, we have seen that the codification of written English has been more widespread, and more effective, than any attempts to regularise spoken English.

Exercises

1. Throughout this book, there will be exercises encouraging you to think about the form and function of the varieties of English you encounter on a regular basis. Thinking about your own experience, note down whether you regularly use, hear or read English in the following contexts:

    a. at home
    b. when you are talking with friends
    c. on the local television or radio station
    d. when you read your local newspaper
    e. when you visit your favourite websites
    f. when you send a text message.

If you use or encounter a language or languages other than English, which are they, and in which of these contexts do you use them?

2. Now repeat the exercise in (1a), (1b) and (1d), but this time note down whether you use a particular variety of English in the different contexts, and whether you mix between different varieties in the same context. Why do you think you use different varieties in different contexts?

Further reading

For a discussion of the concept 'native speaker', see particularly Davies (2003). Useful discussions about language and dialect are found in most introductory textbooks on sociolinguistics (see references in the further reading section of the introduction). Language attitudes are discussed by Preston (2002), and, in the context of the ideology of Standard English, by Milroy and Milroy (1998).

Notes

1 For brevity's sake, only part of the definitions is given here.

2 For details of transcription conventions and a list of phonetic symbols, see the appendix.

2 Communities, networks and individuals

2.1 Overview

In the previous chapter, we looked at some of the ways in which the concepts of 'the English language' and 'dialects of English' have been described and categorised. One of the things we considered was that speaking English (and speaking a dialect of English) are markers of identity, so that the very notion of 'English' may be a social concept, because it is associated with (groups of) people. In this chapter, we focus on the speaker dimension in greater detail, by considering how speakers of a variety of English might be categorised. Do they form a well-defined community, with clear demarcations between groups? Or are individuals linked in an open-ended network, with one community blurring into the next? What kinds of communities use English, and for what kinds of purposes? These and similar questions will be addressed in this chapter.

2.2 What is a community?

A community is something more than simply a random collection of individuals. A community has a shape and a structure, which is internally cohesive and externally distinctive. Members of a community must have enough in common to be identifiable (both to others within the group and to external observers) as members of that community, and must show enough differences from non-members to indicate that they do not belong to any other contrasting communities.

Membership of a community can be both voluntary and enforced, though enforced membership is rare, and arises usually as a result of dependence on others: for example, children in many societies have no option but to be members of a particular community, but as they age, and begin to establish their own sense of identity and distinctiveness, their allegiance to that community may change. Much more common

16

is voluntary community membership, where individuals come together because they have shared practices, beliefs or knowledge.

Part of this knowledge may be linguistic, and the concept of a shared language can help a community to achieve social cohesion. As we saw in the previous chapter, speaking the same language is one way of indicating identity with some and distinctiveness from others: speakers of English are 'like' other speakers of English and 'not like' speakers of French or Telugu. A potential issue here is that the vast majority of the world's population are not monolingual, so bilingual French–English speakers in Canada or Telugu–English speakers in India either (a) are members of two communities at the same time (which blurs the distinctiveness of each community); (b) are members of one community when they speak English and another community when they speak French or Telugu (which means that they are not members of one community exclusively, unlike the monolinguals, which has repercussions for the 'identity' issue); or (c) are members of an entirely different community, that of the bilingual speaker (which would, on grounds of cohesion and distinctiveness, suggest that there is no overlap with either of the monolingual communities, which seems counterintuitive). But the extent of this problem is greatly magnified by the fact that such a conception of the speech community is one that is based exclusively on speech (Lyons 1970: 326), and identification of a group of individuals as a community based on speech alone may be problematic, as we shall see below.

One definition of a speech community we will not be pursuing here (though we will return to it in the final chapter) is one which idealises away from issues of real language use, and focuses on the 'perfect' speaker of a language in a community which admits of no variation (Chomsky 1965). Such an ideal has been important in work on other aspects of language (particularly a variant of formal linguistic theory), but is not concerned primarily with language in use, which has been of paramount importance in much sociolinguistic theorising.

2.3 The English speech community and social networks

Can we define the English speech community simply as the people who speak English? This does not seem problematic at first; after all, if we talk about a 'farming community', we are simply talking about a group of people who have farming in common (and we are not interested in other features which may or may not make such individuals cohere as a group, such as their interest in rock music or the colour of their eyes). One thing we would want to say about the English speech community is that they all share some sort of common linguistic knowledge. But this may be where our problems start, because it is hard to agree on what such 'knowledge of English' might actually be. We saw in Chapter 1 that trying to define what 'English' is on purely linguistic grounds can be problematic, so using that as a further criterion to establish another definition seems ill-advised. Furthermore, defining a group solely in terms of linguistic behaviour is also problematic. We use more than just language when we identify a series of individuals as belonging to a particular group: we might make reference to clothing, conduct, and so on, so we need to be clear whether or not we want language alone to be the sole criterion for establishing a speech community. To return to our farming community, do we include people who own farms, and not those who work on the farm but do not own it? If we include both, then we are already invoking things other than simply farming as criteria for membership (that is, ownership vs. labour). As Patrick (2002: 576) observes, the notion of the speech community "is evidently fraught with difficulties". In this section, we try to unpack such difficulties in relation to the English speech community, to establish whether and how we might use the concept.

As part of a discussion of an ongoing linguistic change in Philadelphia, Labov (1989: 2, 52) wrote:

(1) The English language is a property of the English speech community, which is in turn composed of many nested subcommunities. There is no doubt that Philadelphia speakers of English are members of the larger community of American English speakers, and the even larger community of all speakers of English . . . Individual behavior can be understood only as a reflection of the grammar of the speech community. Language is not a property of the individual, but of the community. Any description of a language must take the speech community as its object if it is to do justice to the elegance and regularity of linguistic structure.

This draws on an earlier suggestion made by Labov, namely that we require a very specific definition of the speech community in order to explain the regularity in attitudes to linguistic behaviour across speakers of different social classes (Labov 1972: 120–1). However, not all sociolinguists agree with this definition of a speech community (see the comments on Spanish in Texas, Colombia and Spain in Mesthrie et al. 2009: 36). Labov's work (which we will consider in more detail in Chapters 4 and 5) is very important in sociolinguistics generally. Labov has claimed that the critical issue in establishing a speech community is the notion of shared norms: a speech community is defined by consensus on what is and is not appropriate for that community, in terms of particular aspects of language usage.

These norms are arbitrary, may differ radically in one community from those in another, and may change over time. For instance, it once was the case that the pronunciation of /r/ in words like *war* and *ward* was considered the norm for careful (and in some people's views, correct) speech in England; now, absence of /r/ in such words is considered the national norm, while in the United States, the opposite is true. We can see this by comparing results in a British and an American survey which looked at the absence of /r/ in such words across different social classes. The higher the social class, the greater the likelihood that /r/ is retained in these words in New York (Labov 1966), but the *less* the likelihood that /r/ is retained in these words in Norwich (Trudgill 1974). We can see here the essential arbitrariness of prestige variants – what is considered nationally prestigious in America is not nationally prestigious in England, and vice versa. But within each community, there is a consensus, which manifests itself in patterns associated with stylistic variation. We will examine stylistic variation in detail in Chapter 4, but for now it is enough to point out the following observation, based on many sociolinguistic studies which have considered differences in speech associated with speakers' social class and the formality of the discourse: for many linguistic variables, in more formal styles, speakers of all social classes use a higher proportion of the variant that is associated with the upper-middle class.

We can make a parallel with aspects of dress: it happens to be a historical convention that middle-class men in some western communities are more likely to wear a suit and tie going about their daily business, outside the home at least – but all men, irrespective of social class, are more likely to wear a suit and tie on formal occasions (like weddings or job interviews). The community as a whole has agreed on this behaviour – it is arbitrary (there is no inherent need to wear a suit and tie at a job interview; it is simply conventional to do so), and operates across the community. Some sociolinguistic studies (for example, Cheshire 1982) have revealed that not everyone may adhere to the equivalent linguistic norms, so some informants (known as outliers) may continue to use local pronunciations or grammatical constructions even in the most formal contexts, just as some people might wear jeans and a t-shirt to a job interview – but such behaviour is atypical.

An interesting point to raise here concerns the persistence of non-standard forms, given the power associated with standard language. Why do non-standard accents and dialects persist, given that studies of style-shifting have shown that speakers do have the capacity to use standard variants in particular discourse contexts? Again, our dress analogy is useful – sometimes people simply don't want to wear a suit and tie, they want to wear jeans and a t-shirt (possibly because their friends and family typically wear such clothes), so they identify more readily with one style of dress – the style they feel most comfortable in most of the time – but recognise that on occasion they need to change to fit the appropriate social context. Similarly, people may continue to use non-standard language because of the associations it has with the other people with whom they interact.

Although the dress analogy helps to illustrate these points, there is an important difference between dress codes and linguistic norms. It is probably more likely that dress codes are established through comment and (where necessary) correction than is the case with linguistic norms. Certainly there are some occasions where violation of a linguistic norm is subject to comment, often from a caregiver or teacher to a child; but in many cases, linguistic norms are established subconsciously by exposure to ordinary language in different discourse contexts. Note too that the norms that are established in a community may be associated with widespread or with local models of behaviour. Widespread norms are the ones which govern behaviour in more formal contexts, and linguistic variants associated with such contexts are said to have overt prestige – Standard English is governed by such norms, so Standard English typically has overt prestige. But the local norms governing linguistic behaviour may also have prestige for particular groups, even if this is not overtly recognised. This has come to be known as covert prestige, and covert prestige – loyalty to vernacular norms – has been seen as an important factor in resisting the advance of the standard variety.

Furthermore, what we witness in such cases of social and stylistic stratification of variation in language is that the variation is not random, but structured (what is sometimes described as "orderly heterogeneity", Weinreich et al. 1968: 100). Such group uniformity is critical in Labov's conception of the speech community; most critical is the fact that both orderly heterogeneity and shared norms are crucial for a group of speakers to be considered a speech community.

Clearly such a claim has great repercussions for our understanding of English (and varieties of English). Crucially, the claim that linguistic knowledge is shared demotes the individual and promotes the group. 'English' is not something that any individual knows; it is a 'property' of the group, not of any member of the group in isolation. Furthermore, agreement on a set of shared norms suggests a consensus view of society, that all members of a speech community agree on a set of shared norms.

A partial challenge to this view has been proposed by sociolinguists who work with the concept of the social network (Milroy 1992; Milroy 2002). As is the case with the speech community, sociolinguists use the term 'social network' in a number of ways, but the following features are usually accepted in most definitions. Essential to the concept of the social network is the idea that individuals contract social bonds with other individuals. Such bonds vary in strength: the social bond between mother and child is typically stronger than that between a shop assistant and his customer. Strong sectors of networks – where many individuals all know each other (that is, the network is dense) and are connected to one another via a series of bonds (family, kinship, employment etc., meaning the network is multiplex) – are typically resistant to changes; weak sectors (where few individuals know one another and/or where individuals are connected via only one bond) may serve to bridge a series of strong sectors in the larger network web.

One of the beauties of network analysis is that it is applicable in all communities (since all humans contract some kind of social bond, to some degree, with other humans). In western communities, strong networks are often found at either end of the class spectrum, with weak networks characterising the middle classes. This intersection of network and social class is highly relevant to our discussion of the speech community. In work on Belfast English (for example, Milroy 1992), it was argued that strong working-class networks have rather different norms from strong upper-class networks (with middle-class networks rather caught in between, with some loyalties to both). Furthermore, it was clear that disruption to the social fabric of the network correlated with linguistic changes (particularly the incursion of supra-local forms into a group of speakers who regularly used vernacular variants). This points not to a consensus model of social class, but rather to a conflict model. The different norms held by different networks suggest a number of things:

- Norms (both social and linguistic) are regulated at highly local levels.
- Different norms held by a working-class community may explain the persistence of non-standard varieties of English, despite the wider cultural dominance of the standard variety.
- Social changes which may disrupt strong network ties will allow for linguistic changes to take place and/or a shift in the distribution of variants across other social groupings within the various networks (for example, males and females, or members of different ethnic groups).

The social network model therefore poses a challenge to Labov's conception of the English speech community, since it argues for a series of subgroups of English speakers, who hold differing (and perhaps even opposing) norms. Gumperz (1996) proposes a model in which aspects of linguistic behaviour are said to be connected to social meaning in some way. In this model, speakers might use a variety of English in order to index a series of social relationships in the group. We will explore this in more detail in Chapter 4, but it is important to raise this here as it provides us with another way of thinking about a speech community. Essentially, such a way of thinking suggests that a speech community is something that groups of individual speakers do, something created by speakers as they negotiate aspects of their identity through language: it is aligned with the social meaning of linguistic variation. Furthermore, the boundary around the speech community may be rather ill-defined, when we consider Gumperz' observation that speech communities "broadly conceived, can be regarded as collectives of social networks" (Gumperz 1996: 362). One suggestion about the speech community, therefore, is that it is not a pre-existing construct, but rather the result of a particular set of linguistic activities.

2.4 Communities of practice

Communities of practice are defined by three particular characteristics: mutual engagement, a jointly negotiated enterprise, and a shared repertoire (Wenger 1998; see also Eckert and McConnell-Ginet 1992a). An example of a community of practice is a school rock band. Here, a number of individuals come together in face-to-face contact (mutual engagement) for a particular purpose, that is, to play music (jointly negotiated enterprise), often conversing using jargon common in discourse on popular music, such as *riff, bridge, amp, bass guitar* and so on (shared repertoire). In fact, many other adolescent groups can legitimately be considered communities of practice because they involve what Meyerhoff (2002: 528) describes as "a process of social learning" (see further Lave and Wenger 1991); and the reason they involve such social learning is that communities of practice are essentially agentive, by which I mean they constitute forums through which individuals exercise aspects of their identity volitionally. Speakers learn the associations of language and identity in part through the social practices they engage in as members of specific communities of practice. Unlike in the cases of the other two kinds of community we have so far considered – the speech community and the social network – members of a community of practice are by definition motivated to belong to that community.

What can this tell us about a community of English speakers? An important point about communities of practice is that language is only one of the resources upon which speakers draw in order to carry out social learning; conversely, communities of practice are defined by much more than just language (cf. the earlier discussion of a speech community). Communities of practice are none the less very useful ways of exploring how particular dialect variants in English come to have the social meaning that they do, because in communities of practice, particular linguistic variants become part of a range of resources that individuals use to negotiate aspects of their identity, with others in the same community of practice, and with yet others who are outwith that community. In other words, a particular feature of the community-of-practice approach to linguistic variation is that it seeks to embed local displays of identity and negotiation of social meaning within larger categories such as networks and speech communities.

An example of this comes from a high school in the north-west of England. Moore (2004) discusses grammatical variation in two communities of practice at the school, by examining the behaviour of two groups of girls labelled the 'Populars' and the 'Townies'. The latter group emerges as a distinct community of practice through participation in a number of behaviours (such as drug taking) and displays (such as style of clothing), and the study illustrates the linguistic correlates of the emergence of this group through a real-time observation of the communities: as the 'Townie' group becomes more distinct in other aspects of its social practice, so it begins to diverge from the 'Popular' group in terms of the proportion of some of the non-standard grammatical variants it uses. For instance, in the north-west (and other) areas of England, the use of *were* with a first or third person singular subject (for example, *I were, he were, the boy were*) is non-standard, and, as they aged, the Townies showed a significant increase in the use of this variant compared to members of the Popular group. However, with other variables (such as right-node raising, as in *He's really stupid, Billy*, where the noun phrase (here *Billy*) to which the pronoun (*he*) is linked appears after the pronoun itself), there was no such divergence between the two groups – so not all instances of non-standard grammar were being used by the Townies in the same way. Other linguistic factors might be relevant here (such as the degree of deviance of the two sets of variables – non-standard *were* is subject to more overt stigma than right-node raising, so variation with the latter is perhaps more acceptable). Taken together, we can see how in these communities of practice, different patterns indicate some of the ways in which linguistic variation can acquire social meaning (often as a product of the interactional purposes of any given communicative event). Particularly, the study illustrates manipulation of the same variables by different groups in order to negotiate different meanings by signalling different social identities.

2.5 Virtual communities

The kinds of communities we have been discussing so far are those which often involve a great deal of face-to-face contact, where members are physically present. As technology has evolved, the possibilities for communication where speaker and audience may be located in any place in the world have increased, and this has correlated with some significant changes to particular varieties of English. An important arena for the development of 'new Englishes' (see Chapter 7) is the web and other electronic media. A study of electronic English (or e-English) reveals interesting patterns of relevance for our understanding of communities and variation. One of the ways in which e-English has emerged as a new variety concerns changes in English orthography, or spelling, and punctuation. As we saw in Chapter 1, the standardisation of English has been most successful in terms of the spelling system: there is now far greater consensus across users of English in the spelling of a word like *hour* than there is in its pronunciation, for example. There has, however, always been variation in spelling, both as a reflection of different ways of pronouncing words (as we see in current dialect literature, for example), or as a result of particular printing practices (in the mid-eighteenth century, many printers capitalised all nouns, as is the case in modern German, but this practice fell away towards the end of the century). What is interesting about text messaging (SMS) in English is the way in which standard practices are variably ignored (because they are not policed in the same way), so that some text messages appear with no capital letters, no punctuation, abbreviations, use of numerals to represent a series of sounds, and so on (for example, *c u 2nite luv g*).

Use of mobile/cell phones and the internet forms part of a more general history in which the development of technology correlates with changes in the history of English. This is not restricted merely to communication technology (such as the development of printing, radio, and television), but is true of other kinds of technology which facilitated face-to-face communication over increasingly wide areas (aeroplanes, cars, and even the humble bicycle). What is special about e-English, however, is the rapidity and extent of its spread, and – focusing more on its formal properties – the way in which it blends aspects of spoken and written communication.

Some features of electronic communication are not restricted to the use of English: for example, smileys such as ☺ can be used as politeness markers in an attempt by the sender of the message to mitigate the force of an imposition contained elsewhere in the correspondence. Similarly, some of the properties of communication more generally – such as turn-taking, interruptions, and overlaps – which have been widely studied by discourse analysts, can be significantly different in computer-mediated discourse, but again this is not really an issue of English (apart from the fact that most people communicate in English). A further issue is the nature of the imposition of norms on the language used. E-English is not subject to the kind of filtering that occurs with other written texts: the text you are reading now has been reviewed and revised a number of times, proof-read, copy-edited and so on. This is not standard procedure for a number of web-based publications, particularly in blogs and chatrooms. In this regard, e-English is much more like spoken than written language. Spoken language can be edited in a way – there are false starts, and repairs, in ordinary conversation – but it is not possible to delete an utterance: once it's out, it's out. Furthermore, the policing of norms of e-English is paradoxically similar to and different from that of spoken English. It is clear that there are rules governing how language is used online (known as *netiquette*), but it is only significant breaches of accepted use that are overtly commented on; the somewhat impersonal nature of online discourse means that fewer features of identity are overtly marked. At the same time, it is clear that particular traits of individuals do surface when looking at a corpus of online discourse, so there is evidence that individual styles emerge in this variety of English, just as they do in ordinary face-to-face communication.

2.6 The individual

So far we have discussed the language associated with groups of speakers; in this section, the focus is on the individual. Individual linguistic knowledge is not much discussed in sociolinguistics, though there are some exceptions (see particularly Hudson 1996); usually, the linguistic knowledge of the individual is associated with formal linguistics. Yet clearly, all of the groups we have been discussing are groups of individual speakers, each with her or his own linguistic experience (which cannot be shared with anyone else – no one on earth has exactly the same linguistic experience as you do). What reasons are there for and against focusing on the language of the individual in sociolinguistics?

One argument that has been proposed against a focus on the individual over the community has been that the individual shows great irregularity and numerous idiosyncrasies compared to the group – the behaviour of the group shows how regular patterns of linguistic variation and change are (Gumperz 1982). For example, outliers by their very nature do not correspond to group norms, and so, because they don't fit the generalisation, we need to recognise them as special and discount them. Only group patterns reflect the orderly heterogeneity of linguistic variation (and the patterned way in which language changes). An argument in favour of basing generalisations on individuals is that each individual constitutes a well-defined variety, if we follow Hudson's definition of a variety as a "*set of linguistic items with similar social distribution*" (Hudson 1996: 22, emphasis original). Indeed, it is difficult to think of a better-defined correlation between language system and language user, if one accepts that the language system of an individual is unique to that individual. However, this too is a contentious claim (some sociolinguists and some theoretical linguists dispute it, though for different reasons) for reasons we will explore in Chapter 9.

2.7 Summary

In this chapter we have looked at the nature of communities, networks and individual speakers of English. We have seen that defining the boundaries around the speech community may be a difficult task, and that traditional work involving the concept of the speech community has been complemented by work involving the networks that speakers choose to be part of (including particular communities of practice). There is little doubt that individuals may be most directly affected by the practices of those most close to them, and results from network studies show that some varieties of English (particular non-standard varieties) are typically used by speakers in strong (that is, dense and multiplex) networks, which are more resistant to the pressure to use Standard English. At the same time, work on speech communities shows how larger groups cohere, and attempt to distinguish themselves from speakers of other varieties. When we attempt to put boundaries around different networks or communities, we run into the same kinds of classificatory difficulties that we saw when we tried to define 'English' as a language. We can only be sure of two kinds of boundary, one social, and one linguistic. The social boundary is the individual speaker (socially unique) and the linguistic boundary is the knowledge of language which that speaker has (linguistically unique). Beyond that, the boundaries become harder to define. This has a number of ramifications for understanding the social dimensions of English as a language, as we will see in later chapters.

Exercises

1. For this chapter, think about the different social bonds you have with particular individuals with whom you form a group of some kind. For example, you could think of your family, a club you belong to, colleagues at work, an online community, and so on. Do you use a particular kind of English with this group? To what extent is this simply a matter of lexical choices? Is there variation in some other aspect of language (such as grammar)?

2. Assuming you are using this book as part of a university course, to what extent do you think your tutorial, seminar or lecture group constitutes a community of practice? (Remember that this is defined by mutual engagement, jointly negotiated enterprise, and a shared repertoire.) If you believe the group does constitute a community of practice, what are the linguistic features of this shared repertoire? If you believe it does not, what particular aspects of the group mean that it is not a community of practice?

Further reading

Patrick (2002) provides an excellent survey of the treatment of the speech community in sociolinguistic theory, while Milroy (2002) and Meyerhoff (2002), in the same publication, give comprehensive accounts of social networks and communities of practice, respectively. Another useful publication on communities of practice is Eckert and McConnell-Ginet (1992a). Hudson (1996) discusses some of the problems associated with speech community as a concept, and argues for a sociolinguistic account focusing on the individual. Crystal (2006c, 2008) provides a good introduction to language, electronic media, and text messaging.

3 English and language planning

3.1 Overview

In Chapter 5, we will look at some of the ways in which variation in English and interaction between speakers may result in language change, where some of the variant forms come to be used less frequently, until they disappear, while new forms replace them. This kind of language change is part of a natural evolution of human languages, arising from ordinary interactional discourse. Sometimes, however, the language of a community may change as the result of particular, organised, and targeted interventions, normally by powerful groups. A government may make a decision that only one or two languages among many should be the medium of education in local state-run schools, so that other languages become restricted in their domains of use; conversely, a media organisation may decide to produce a new newspaper in a language which up to that point had not been used to report local, national and international events, which would increase the domains of use of that language. A grammar of a hitherto unrecorded language might be produced by linguists and local educationalists; conversely, a funding body might decide to limit funding for the production of dictionaries, grammars and other resources in a local language. Such decisions are part of the ebb and flow of organised language change: this is the main business of language planning. In this chapter, we will look at the role of English in language planning; particularly we will consider the following:

- how (standard) English itself was planned in England from the sixteenth through to the eighteenth century, and continues to have an effect to this day in the United Kingdom;
- how the spread of English as a global language has affected language planning in communities across the globe;
- the advantages and disadvantages of having English as the official language of a community.

Before we look in detail at language planning involving English, we will first look more generally at issues involved in language planning.

3.2 How to plan a language

Language planning can involve anything from suggesting that a dictionary like the *Oxford English Dictionary* include a new word through to the imposition of a particular language as the official language of a nation, so it may take very many forms. For instance, in 2009, an English council made a proposal to remove apostrophes from all of the street signs they produced, because of the number of complaints they received about whether or not particular placenames should have an apostrophe, and if so, where it should be (for example, *King's Norton, Kings' Norton* or *Kings Norton*), a decision which was criticised by the Apostrophe Preservation Society. Such a decision counts as an example of language planning, albeit on a small, local scale. The critical issue is that a particular linguistic feature (that is, the apostrophe in the written language) has become restricted in its domains of use (that is, no longer used on street signs). This was not the result of a natural development, agreed on tacitly by members of a speech community; this was an overt decision made by a group who had the power to enforce it.

While the presence or absence of the apostrophe may seem a rather trivial issue (though not, it seems, to the Apostrophe Preservation Society), we can see rather similar processes when a government decides to impose a particular language as the official language in a community. In such cases, other languages may become restricted in their domains of use. For instance, if English is adopted as an official language in communities where many other languages are spoken, those languages may become marginalised because they no longer have the range of functions that they once had: this affects the status of those languages in that community. So, as we see so often in sociolinguistic issues, we need to consider both the question of form (for example, whether or not to use the apostrophe) and the question of function (for example, in what contexts a particular language is to be used). Indeed, any decision on language planning must first confront the following questions: is the purpose of the planning to effect change in the function of the various languages spoken in a community, or is it to effect change in the form of one particular language, or is to effect change in both? The first type of planned change is sometimes referred to as status planning, the second as corpus planning (Kloss 1969).

Status planning, as its name suggests, involves changing the status of one or more languages in a community. One way to do this is to declare a particular language the national language, or the official language, of a country. It is important to note that sociolinguists usually distinguish between a national language and an official language, even if governments do not, and even if the same language functions as both the national and official language of the country. A national language is one which functions very much as an identity marker. It works to strengthen the bond between a community of speakers and a set of linguistic forms (however fuzzy the distinction between different communities and different languages may be, as we saw in the previous chapters). Indeed, to declare a particular variety to be a national language may increase the subjective associations between language and the notion of a 'nation state'. By contrast, an official language has a much less affective function: it is simply a language that is used for governmental, bureaucratic business.

Corpus planning involves changes to particular aspects of linguistic form. Consider in this regard the creation of a dictionary. Imagine you were given the task of creating a dictionary for the variety of English spoken in your local community. First, which words do you decide to include in the dictionary, and which do you discard? How do you spell those words? How much consensus across the community does there need to be in the definition of the word? Do you include words that are only used by the elder members of your community? (If you do, when those people die, your dictionary will include obsolete words; if you don't, you'll lose the opportunity to create an archive of your variety which made it distinctive.) Do you include very new words, used by teenagers, even if the particular meaning for that word may be short-lived? (In the 1980s, some speakers of English used the word *bad* to mean 'good', but fewer people do now, including the people who used it when they were teenagers.) These, and many others, are relevant questions involved in planning the lexicon of a particular variety, and the same kinds of questions will be relevant to anyone planning the grammar of the variety too.

While it is important to distinguish corpus planning and status planning, it would be wrong to think that one does not affect the other. The creation of a dictionary of your variety (corpus planning) has an effect on what is considered to be a feature of your variety, and what is not, and also suggests something about how that variety might be regarded both by members of your community and by members of other communities, namely that it is 'good' enough, and distinctive enough, to warrant a dictionary of its own: these are matters typically associated with status planning. And the label one gives to a dictionary also reflects the status of the variety it describes: compare the *Dictionary of Smoky*

Mountain English (Montgomery and Hall 2004) with the *Dictionary of the Scots Language* (www.dsl.ac.uk), where the former implicitly suggests that what is described is a dialect of English, and the latter explicitly denotes Scots to be a language separate from English.

We can also add the following to the list of ways of planning a language: prestige planning and acquisition planning (see further Lo Bianco 2004). Prestige planning is more concerned with language attitudes; particularly, it is concerned with engendering, at a community level, positive attitudes towards the variety that is being selected. So while both status planning and prestige planning are concerned with the perceived value of a variety, they differ in that status planning is concerned with establishing appropriate functions for a variety (whether it should be used in religious ceremonies, in schools, in parliament and so on), while prestige planning is concerned with establishing a positive regard for the variety in the society which will be expected to use it in an extended set of functions. Acquisition planning is usually educational in focus, and involves the decisions made about what language or languages should be (a) the medium of education and/or (b) the subject of education in a community.

What motivates individuals, and groups of individuals, to plan a language? Given the associations between language and nationhood, we might suspect that some attempts at planning are politically motivated. For instance, a group may decide to adopt English as an official language, and to insist that English is the medium of education, in order to create opportunities for its citizens to gain access to the currently dominant global language; by contrast, a local language might be raised in status to a national language, in order to promote local identity in opposition to the globalisation of English, and to distinguish that nation from others nearby. In other words, motivations for language planning may stem from perceived problems in the society, which may be addressed by changes to the form and/or function of a particular language, or set of languages. Not all of these problems are necessarily resolved by governmental intervention: some kinds of language planning may take place at a local and even individual level; furthermore, the planning may not fulfil the political aims. Choosing to avoid what is perceived as politically incorrect language (for example, using the term *chairperson* rather than *chairman*, to avoid inherently sexist language) may be a personal choice, though it may also be promoted by other groups. But at whichever level this is implemented – from individual to national or even supra-national government – it is important to remember that language planning is deliberate, conscious language change. In relation to English, language planning has often been associated with colonising powers, as noted above. But to begin, we consider an early example of language planning: the vernacularisation (Cobarrubias 1983) of English in England.

3.3 Planning English in England

In Chapter 6, we will consider some general aspects of English historical linguistics; in this chapter, we focus particularly on the period from the late fifteenth century onwards, in order to explore some of the ways in which English was planned in England. It is sometimes tempting to think of English in language planning as an issue which only applies to the spread of English beyond the British Isles (and associated with the political and economic dominance of the United Kingdom and the United States of America in the nineteenth and twentieth centuries). But it is important to realise that language planning was a feature of English in England too.

From the Norman Conquest to the fifteenth century, English was not held in very high esteem in England, as far as government, education and science were concerned. As England grew in political power, first in Europe, then further afield, so support grew for the promotion of the vernacular language as the proper language for government (an example of status planning); but in order to achieve this, it was recognised that there also had to be an overt, planned, standard variety (an example of corpus planning). The selection of that standard variety was linguistically arbitrary, but socially and politically motivated. In the sixteenth century, as the English nation (and empire) began to establish itself on the world stage, there was a rise in nationalist feeling which provoked debate on the status of the English language: a clear link between language and nationhood was established. Particularly, there were comparisons between the vernacular language English, and the supra-local, high-status language Latin:

(1) I love Rome, but London better, I favour Italy, but England more, I honour the Latin, but I worship the English (Mulcaster, Peroration to *The Elementarie*, 1582)

While there was support for the promotion of English as the national language, it was clear that the diversity of dialects within England meant that one particular variety would need to be selected, as noted above. In advising poets which variety of English should be used, the author of the *Arte of English Poesie* (published in 1589), thought to be George Puttenham, suggested a particular regional variety:

(2) ye shall therefore take the vsuall speach [= usual speech] of the Court, and that of London and the shires lying about London within lx. Myles [= 60 miles], and not much aboue [= above].

and a particular social variety:

(3) neither shall he [= the poet] follow the speach of a craftes man or carter, or other of the inferiour sort, though he be inhabitant or bred in the best towne and Citie in this Realme, for such persons doe abuse good speaches by strange accents . . . he shall follow generally the better brought vp sort . . . men ciuill [= civil] and graciously behauoured [=behaved] and bred.

It was not by chance that the London dialect was selected as the standard variety – although not inherently better, more elegant, or more suited to the purpose, it was the variety spoken by the social elite and the politically powerful.

Once selected, the variety had to be codified in various ways. Codification is a critical part of the standardisation process since it is this stage which is crucial in attempting to eliminate variation. The true measure of success of a standard variety is absence of variation – if there is no phonological or grammatical variation, it is not possible for one pronunciation or grammatical structure to be rated higher than another – and codification is concerned with establishing what counts as standard and what counts as non-standard, by regularising spellings, pronunciations, words and grammar. It is typically the case that variation in pronunciation is more tolerated than variation in spelling, grammar and vocabulary, so much so that Haugen (1987) identifies three kinds of processes involved in codification, none of which includes regulation of accent variation: graphisation (which aims at developing a writing system, and increasing uniformity in the written language), grammatication (reduction in variation in grammar by establishing a set of overt rules) and lexicalisation (fixing the wordstock of a language). Such regularisation is attempted by the production of:

- dictionaries, like that of Samuel Johnson, published in 1755, and the later *Oxford English Dictionary*;
- grammars, such as *The Rudiments of English Grammar* (by Joseph Priestley, published in 1761) and *A Short Introduction to English Grammar* (by Robert Lowth, published in 1762);
- usage manuals, and guides to proper pronunciation, such as *Errors of Pronunciation, and Improper Expressions, used frequently, and chiefly by the*

Inhabitants of London (an anonymous publication which appeared in 1817).

The fact that guides to proper pronunciation emerge in the eighteenth and nineteenth centuries suggests that the selected variety had become accepted by a wider community (such that people who didn't speak it were made aware of their 'errors'); and the fact that such books, and many others, of many different genres, were written in the standard language suggests that it had undergone an elaboration of function. Thus the planning of English in England meets Haugen's criteria for the standardisation of a language: selection, codification, elaboration, and acceptance (Haugen 1966).

Two other aspects of language planning are relevant to the development of Standard English in the United Kingdom and beyond. We can say of Standard English that it emerged as a product of prestige planning. This involves more than change to linguistic form; it involves encouraging change in attitudes towards a language, particularly one which historically was marginalised. In other words, it involves particular political and social motivation to bring about a change. To a certain extent, we saw this in the quotations from Mulcaster and Puttenham above, but they were primarily concerned with particular disputes about the status of English in relation to Latin, and which of the possible varieties of English should be selected as the standard one. Below is an example of a seventeenth-century text which explicitly illustrates prestige planning (note that in cases where the <u> letter appears between vowels, contemporary standard English would have a <v> letter (for example, <improued> means 'improved'):

(4) our language [that is, English] is improued aboue all others now spoken by any nation, and became the fairest, the nimblest, the fullest; most apt to vary the phrase, most ready to receiue good composition, most adorned with sweet words and sentences, with witty quips and ouer-ruling Prouerbs: yea, able to express any hard conceit whatsoeuer with great dexterity: waighty in weighty matters, merry in merry, braue in braue. (William Lisle, Preface to *A Saxon Treatise*, 1623, cited in Barber 1997: 51)

Notice that Lisle here is not suggesting particular changes to the form of English, nor is he recommending particular functions which English is fit for. Rather, he is simply promoting the language, attempting to encourage favourable attitudes towards a language which was increasingly growing in prestige. Finally, as English developed into an international language in the centuries following Lisle, we see the emergence of acquisition planning, which can involve the promotion of the language as a target in second language acquisition (which, in terms of the promotion of English, is part of the work of organisations such as the British Council). This then leads us to a further issue: language planning and English beyond England.

3.4 English in Kenya, Sri Lanka and the European Union

We move now in time and space, from England in the seventeenth century, to Kenya in the twentieth century. Here we see a different social and linguistic mix, where English is involved in language planning, but where tensions exist between different local languages, and between local languages and English (Simango 2006). Kenya gained independence from the United Kingdom in 1963, having been colonised in the previous century. English was decreed to be an official language in Kenya along with Swahili in 1974. That Swahili was chosen as a co-official language was quite a surprising choice, since few Kenyans spoke that variety, and Swahili was not commonly spoken in the capital, Nairobi. The use of English in official domains (for example, as a medium for education, or as the language typically used by members of the armed forces) has been contentious, and some have called for a vernacularisation policy, such that a language like Kamba or Luo be raised to the status of official language. Reasons in favour of such a move include the fact that the use of English is in some ways an unwelcome reminder of colonial oppression; furthermore, given that speakers of any of the other indigenous languages of Kenya (like Rendille or Samburu) are in something of a lose-lose situation anyway – they have to use something other than their native language, whether that be English or not – there are solid political reasons for selecting two indigenous languages as the official languages of the country. By contrast, others have argued that encouraging the use of English among the population gives Kenyans access to a wider socioeconomic world, with greater employment prospects; and English is in some ways a sensible choice as an official language because, by its very nature as a non-indigenous language, it does not promote the interests of any particular regional group in Kenya. (Of course, it does promote the interests of those who have the easiest access to education, which may mean that use of and exposure to English are determined by social class rather than regional group.)

The relationship between English and other languages in Kenya provides a nice example of the tensions between linguistic assimilation and linguistic pluralism (Cobarrubias 1983). Assimilation involves narrowing, a reduction in variation, sometimes in the hope that promoting a particular language will promote sociopolitical unity. (Notice that this policy is part of the thinking behind encouraging all immigrants to countries like the United Kingdom to be proficient in English – it is seen as part of a citizenship programme.) Pluralism involves the promotion of diversity, whereby a number of languages may be promoted by the state. Again, the motivations for this are usually more than purely linguistic, and have a range of economic consequences. On the one hand, a pluralistic policy encourages multilingualism, and multilingualism may be a valuable economic resource, particularly in a globalised economy; on the other, it can be economically costly to ensure that all varieties are promoted to the same extent, because various educational resources will need to be produced for each language, language teachers will need to be trained to provide instruction in schools, and so on.

In Sri Lanka, issues of language planning arose in the nineteenth century, as part of the expansion of the British Empire. Canagarajah (2005: 421–2) notes that, having taken the island in 1815, the British intended to allow a degree of autonomy to local ethnic groups, but soon realised that a centralised system was essential for optimal governmental business. In order to achieve this, the Colebrook-Cameron commission made recommendations that locals be given training in English so that they could be employed in a series of functionary positions. (Much the same principles seem to have been in operation in a different community almost three hundred years earlier, after the 1536 Act of Union, which resulted in the political marriage of England and Wales. There, Welsh speakers were similarly forced to learn English in order to be appointed to various public offices (Davies 2000: 80).) In nineteenth-century Sri Lanka, not everyone could receive English-medium education: restricting this to a few select individuals was another way of exercising control over the community at large: "English proficiency came to be distributed according to the already prevailing caste hierarchy" (Canagarajah 2005: 422).

Since preference for access to English was also given to Christians and urban dwellers, English quickly acquired the status of a class marker in the wider community. After independence, a rather different language policy was implemented, such that one local language (Sinhala) was accorded official status, though Tamil, now used along with Sinhala as a medium of education, was not. The political situation in Sri Lanka involved great tension between Tamil and Sinhalese groups, and with the rise of Sinhala, many Tamils looked to English to contest the dominance of Sinhala, in addition to promoting Tamil itself. Canagarajah (2005) shows that this has resulted in a very complex linguistic situation in Sri Lanka, where divisions both between and within different ethnic groups have led to repeated fluctuations in language policy, with different groups promoting different languages. The Sri Lankan situation also suggests a blurring of the relationship between ethnicity, language and nation, with speakers recasting the same language in different lights for different social, political and economic ends. And the kind of English used in Sri Lanka is also localised: global English is by no means uniform, and each of the varieties of English used by different speakers is constructed differently by different groups.

English also has an official role to play in the European Union (EU). Despite the fact that the EU promotes multilingualism via translators and interpreters, so that political decisions are made available to individuals in member states where English is not the first language of most speakers, it is still the case that the majority of the documents of the European Commission are first drafted in English, with only a handful drafted in other languages. This political organisation, then, has made a distinction between working languages (in the case of the European Commission, these are English, French and German) and official languages. In fact, English is only one of twenty-three official languages of the EU (as of 2007), and the regulation determining language use in the EU appears actively to promote linguistic pluralism. For instance, article 2 of the Regulation determining the languages to be used by the European Economic Community states that "Documents which a Member State or a person subject to the jurisdiction of a Member State sends to institutions of the Community may be drafted in any one of the official languages selected by the sender. The reply shall be drafted in the same language."

However, in addition to the twenty-three official languages, there are also well over a hundred minority languages in Europe. These too are supported and (to a degree) promoted by the EU, some more so than others. Some languages are not formally recognised by the EU, despite being spoken by approximately one in every fifty people in a particular member state; for example, Turkish in Belgium. As for English, it was not always an official language of the EU: when greater economic co-operation between European states was proposed in the 1950s, the UK was not part of the initial group, so the first four official languages of the precursor of the EU were Dutch, French, Italian and German; and it is still the case that, in terms of first languages, there are more speakers of German than of English in the member states that currently make up the EU. However, when we include reasonably proficient users of English as a second or other language, the ranking changes, and English becomes the most widely spoken language: this also seems to be on the increase, with more and more younger people becoming proficient in English. Over time, then, English has grown to be more and more dominant within the EU. This is part of a larger spread of global English, which raises an important question, addressed in the next section.

3.5 How has the globalisation of English affected language planning?

At the time of writing, English is one of the world's languages (including, for example, Mandarin Chinese and Spanish) which is currently gaining in numbers of speakers as either a first or other language. In some ways, the spread of English is to be welcomed, but in others, there is a real danger that the domination of a few languages will lead to the demise of many others. In this section, we explore some of the ways in which global English is beneficial for communities, and some of the ways in which it is detrimental.

What might be some of the disadvantages of using English as an official language? One issue concerns the perceived status of English in the community, or, more accurately, the perceived status of users of English. If it is the case that English is perceived as the language of an elite, it may be the case that there is some resentment towards using that variety as, for example, the medium of education, because it will automatically privilege an already privileged group, and serve to marginalise those who do not come to education with the added advantage of having a good command of the medium of instruction. A further issue concerns the vitality of indigenous languages. If English comes to be used in wider and wider domains, the motivation for speakers to continue to use indigenous varieties may be marginalised and reduced, sometimes to the point of extinction. The loss of such languages has serious repercussions for the preservation of the cultures of various groups around the world.

Spolsky (2004: 91) has argued that "English as a global language is now a factor that needs to be taken into account in its language policy by any nation state". An important issue in situations of language planning concerns the rights of minority language speakers. There are clearly advantages in promoting minority languages in different countries. For example, such languages can provide an insight into human culture which is lost when those languages are lost. However, critics of those who promote minority language rights suggest that protecting those languages is a wild-goose chase, and even of questionable morality: speakers of those languages want access to the resources, and the power, that come with command of a global language. If they are denied access to such resources, by having their potential exposure to English limited, they are denied the opportunity for socioeconomic growth. Recent work by sociolinguists in Malaysia (David and Govindasamy 2005) and in Iran (Riazi 2005), for example, has suggested that members of some communities feel quite resentful when a local language is promoted to the detriment of English.

By contrast, research in other countries has shown that in situations where English is promoted, sometimes by the use of an English-only policy in some schools (in parts of Eritrea (Wright 2001) and India (Annamalai 2005), for example), educators have tried to find ways around the stated policy and attempting to use local languages in particular ways. Similarly, the addition of English as a further linguistic resource may not involve loss, but rather gain, because while it may be the case that certain languages become marginalised in such circumstances, many speakers may use English as a way of marking particular aspects of their local identity. In such cases, 'English' no longer symbolises a global phenomenon; it becomes part of a local negotiation of social roles and relationships. Furthermore, as Ferguson (2006) observes, it is not the case that language shift is always towards English: many indigenous languages are lost because of shift to other local regional languages. This, in connection with a 'deanglicisation' of English (Kachru 1985), may mean that, in the case of the spread of English, the associations of linguistic form with particular political and social ideologies become reduced, and new associations emerge which have social meaning at a more prominently local level.

3.6 Summary

Crystal (2003), in his discussion of the spread of global English, makes reference to the political and economic might of two empires: that of the United Kingdom in the nineteenth century, and the United States in the twentieth and twenty-first centuries. This power is exercised in a number of ways, and much research currently focuses on matters of economics, particularly as this relates to globalisation. But it is imperative to realise that brute force had – and in some cases, continues to have – an impact on the success of language planning, whether the intention be to promote English, or to promote a local language: we saw that this was particularly the case in the situation in Sri Lanka. By comparing some of the issues associated with the planning of English in England, and the planning of English in other contexts around the world, we see what is constant and what is variable in language planning. Some factors do remain constant (for example, the importance of prestige planning in ensuring wider acceptance of a particular variety); but factors may vary considerably, given the different social, political and economic contexts in which language planning takes place. This is part of the reason why, despite attempts to understand global practices in relation to planning, a deep knowledge of the local socioeconomic and political practices is vital in the development of a workable policy.

Exercise

Choose a country where English has had a role to play in language policy, and try to find out some of the ways in which status planning and corpus planning have been implemented. To what extent has vernacularisation also played a role? If you were in charge of developing policy in this community, how would you ensure that you had sufficient knowledge of the sociolinguistic situation in the community? What factors might limit your ability to discover this sociolinguistic situation?

Further reading

Spolsky (2004) is a detailed account of many issues in language policy, while Ferguson (2006) provides a broad coverage of the relationship between aspects of language planning and educational policy and practice. Phillipson (1992, 2003) links many aspects of language policy to political imperialism with regard to the spread of English within Europe, and further afield. Another useful book specifically on English in this regard is Pennycook (1994). On global English, Bauer (2002) and Crystal (2003) each provide a good introduction, which can be followed up by reference to various articles in Kachru et al. (2006), and to Jenkins (2003) and Schneider (2007).

4 Regional and social variation

4.1 Overview

In the first three chapters, we explored some of the functions of English in communities across the world. In this chapter, the attention is less on the function of varieties of English, and more on their formal properties. Many sociolinguists argue that the function of a particular utterance or discourse will be an influence on the form or shape that the utterance or discourse will take, so we will still need to take function into consideration when we examine why particular varieties of English have the shape that they do. Much of the chapter is devoted to quantitative (also known as variationist) sociolinguistics, but we begin by considering regional variation in English.

As we saw in Chapter 1, for many people, the concept of a variety of English is regionally based: people think of the English-speaking world as being divided up into distinct geographical areas, each with its own dialect. Sometimes this corresponds to a group of nations (for example, Euro English), sometimes to an individual nation (for example, Indian English), and sometimes to an area within a nation, either urban (for example, Boston English) or rural (for example, Lancashire English). These regional dialects are said to have their own distinctive pronunciation, grammar and vocabulary. For instance, some speakers of English from Auckland, New Zealand, have a different vowel in words like *trap* and *cat* (that is, [trɛp] and [kɛt]) from that of some speakers of English from York, England (who have [trap] and [kat]); speakers in San Francisco might introduce a report of somebody else's speech by saying *He was all* (as in *he was all, 'What do you want?'*), while speakers in London might say *This is him* (as in *this is him, 'What do you want?'*).

But such a set of divisions is slightly misleading. It is certainly not the case that all eight million inhabitants of London have *This is him* as a quotative construction. For instance, some Londoners are recent immigrants to the United Kingdom, who have English as a second or other language, whose English is different in form from those born in the English capital; but even those who were born in London, and have English as their first language, display different varieties of English. The language of an elderly white woman from the wealthy suburb of Kensington shows differences from that of a young black man from a poorer area such as Tower Hamlets. And this pattern is replicated in many communities in which English is spoken – the variation in form is not simply a product of the region in which the speakers are located. The social characteristics of the speaker (their class, gender and ethnicity, for instance), the kind of talk they are engaged in, and the audience they are speaking to can all be influential in helping us to understand why varieties of English have the shape that they do.

In terms of the history of research into varieties of English, regional dialectology predates social dialectology. We will see in Chapter 6, when we consider aspects of English historical sociolinguistics, that attitudes towards different regional varieties of English have been expressed for a great time, and that there have been some attempts to describe the formal characteristics of regional varieties of British English since the early Modern English period. But systematic studies of regional varieties of English – that is, studies which used an extensive sample of speakers, and collected data using a fairly uniform methodology – are not found until the twentieth century, and were first carried out in the United Kingdom and in the United States. It is important to understand both the aims and the methods of these traditional dialectologists, since they were the precursors to the sociolinguists whose work we will be investigating in detail in the remainder of the book.

4.2 Aims and methods of traditional dialectologists

In the past, traditional dialectologists were historical linguists; while they had a general interest in modern varieties of English, one specific aim for many traditional dialectologists was the recording of a particular kind of dialect in order to track the outcome of historical sound changes. This meant that they needed to select speakers whose speech was considered to represent 'pure' dialect, uncontaminated by the standard variety. Such speakers are referred to in the literature as NORMs, an acronym meaning Non-mobile, Older, Rural Males (Chambers and Trudgill 1998). It is interesting to note that the opposite 'type' of speaker – young, urban, mobile females (who we might call YUMFs) – have been the focus of much modern sociolinguistic inquiry. Once selected, the NORMs were asked very specific questions, usually using a questionnaire which was as uniform as possible in order to provide

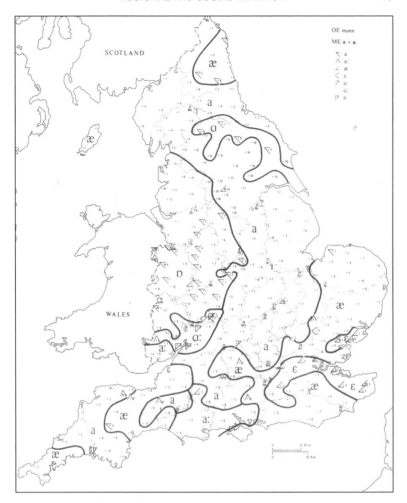

Figure 4.1 Map taken from the *Linguistic Atlas of England* showing variation in pronunciation of the vowel in the word *man*.

consistency across the sample size, to elicit particular responses. These responses allowed the researchers to record the distribution of particular lexical items, and to see how the pronunciation of particular vowels and consonants varied in different parts of the country under investigation. These data were then presented in dialect maps, which divided the land mass into specific regions where particular lexical items or pronunciations were recorded. Figure 4.1, created from data taken from the *Survey of English Dialects* (*SED*, Orton et al. 1962–71), provides an

Figure 4.2 Traditional dialect areas of England (Trudgill 1999a: 34).

example of such a dialect map. It shows the differences in pronunciation of the vowel in the word *man* in various areas of England.

The lines on this map are referred to as isoglosses (from Greek, meaning 'same tongue'), which were used to establish major dialect areas of a language in a particular country. Using a range of *SED* data, Trudgill (1999a) produced a composite map showing the various isoglosses which determined the traditional dialect areas of England, as shown in Figure 4.2.

More recent regional dialectological work has been able to make use of advances in technology. While *SED* researchers sometimes relied on aural transcription, making notes at the point of recording, modern dialectologists use digital recorders to record speakers, and computers to store, process and present the data so collected. For instance, a recent survey of accents of American English (Labov et al. 2005) has produced a digital resource which allows researchers to hear the original recordings. You can also hear a number of different accents of English by visiting the Sound Comparisons website (www.soundcomparisons.com).

4.3 Aims and methods of variationist sociolinguists

While the traditional dialectologists were interested in recording a very specific kind of speaker in a fairly formal style, variationist sociolinguists typically collect data from a range of informants in a range of speech styles (from casual conversation to reading specific words). Such a method allows the researcher to do many things. First, he or she can (using a range of statistical tests) establish what aspects of a speaker's social make-up correlate with the use of particular linguistic forms. For instance, if the speaker sample contains speakers of different ethnicities and social classes, it is possible to establish whether ethnicity or class (or both, or neither) is associated with using a particular linguistic variant or set of variants. Second, the researcher can also investigate the effects of speech style on the kind of language used. One of the earliest findings of variationist sociolinguistics is that speakers in certain communities (typically urban, western communities) will use variants associated with the local vernacular more frequently in casual conversation, and less frequently in formal speech styles (Labov 1966). Third, the researcher can investigate the linguistic behaviour of the individual. For instance, do all speakers in the group investigated behave in the same way, or are there some 'outliers' whose linguistic behaviour is radically different from the rest of the group?

Depending on what kind of research is being undertaken, different methods will be adopted regarding the size of the speaker sample and the nature of the recordings. Some sociolinguistic surveys are carried out using a random sample of informants, who are interviewed using specific questions, and are asked to carry out a variety of linguistic tasks (for example, Labov 1966). Quite a large number of informants can be interviewed in a relatively short period of time, following this method. Other surveys involve a more ethnographic approach, whereby the researcher spends a significant amount of time familiarising herself with the social practices of the community under investigation, and collecting typically informal speech over a long period of time. This kind of research may involve years of observation, and can produce rather different results than those collected via a structured interview (see Eckert 2000). These and other methods are often used in sociolinguistic studies, and reveal complementary findings about the relationship between language and society. Although certain aspects of the method are different, there are some things which are common to most quantitative studies. Particularly, quantitative sociolinguists are interested in patterns of variation, and the quantitative distribution of different variants across different groups. In order to characterise the linguistic variation as accurately as possible, sociolinguists make use of the concept of the linguistic variable.

4.4 The linguistic variable

While the aims and methods of traditional dialectologists and variationist sociolinguists are different in many ways, both groups share an interest in understanding patterns of linguistic variation. Before the advent of modern sociolinguistic research, many linguists had believed variation in language to be unstructured, with random groups of speakers retaining random pronunciations. Such pronunciations were characteristic of sound changes in sets of words which reflected the diverse historical influences on the language of the local area. But this was not the case. Possibly the biggest contribution made by quantitative sociolinguistics was one of its earliest contributions: proof that variation in language was not random, but structured – the "orderly heterogeneity" (or structured differences, Weinreich et al. 1968) discussed previously. And that proof came in part from the use of the linguistic variable.

The linguistic variable is a set or, perhaps better, a network of related linguistic forms, or variants. We often see co-variation between linguistic variables and other variables associated with the speaker (for example, the speaker's social affiliation or his or her age), the audience (for example, whether the addressee is an intimate friend or a stranger), and the nature and situation of the communicative act (for example, whether the speaker is giving evidence in court, or talking in a restaurant). Although the selection of any one variant in the network will typically not affect the referential meaning of the word or utterance, the network itself may have salient social meaning. For instance, many speakers of English will pronounce the intervocalic consonant in the word *butter* very differently. Many Americans pronounce *butter* as [bʌɾɚ], while speakers of London English might pronounce *butter* as [bʌʔə]. However, whichever pronunciation is used, the same concept is denoted in each case. In other words, no matter which of the set of variants is selected, the concept referred to remains constant. This is the critical feature of a linguistic variable. We can see similar patterns with lexical variation (different words referring to the same concept), as in the various terms for 'friend' (including *mate, pal, buddy,* and *marra*), and with grammatical variation (different grammatical patterns conveying the same message), illustrated by the following different kinds of negation: *I haven't been to Canberra, I've not been to Canberra, I ain't been to Canberra,* and *I ain't never been to Canberra.* But variants like *butter* as [bʌɾɚ], *buddy,* and *I ain't been to Canberra* may all be linked in the language user's mind to the concept 'American'.

However, as noted above, such variation is not simply typical of different regions – indeed, some patterns (like the negation example) may be more typical of social varieties than they are of regional varieties. Since variation is characteristic of individuals, we have to recognise that knowledge of variation is part of an individual's knowledge about their own language system – one of the things that speakers know about language is that it varies, so we need a method of representation for that systematic knowledge.

The method of representation we will use in this book is as follows: the linguistic variable (that is, the network of forms) is enclosed in round brackets, and any variants (that is, the members of that network) under discussion follow the variable, separated by a colon. For instance, in many varieties of British English, there is a phenomenon known as H-Dropping, which denotes absence of the glottal fricative [h] at the beginning of words such as *happy, hill* and *house.* But H-Dropping is not invariable: a speaker might sometimes retain the fricative in such words in a more formal style, while we might hear the same speaker pronouncing the same words without an [h] in a more casual style. We therefore have a variable (h), with two variants, namely (h):[h] and (h):ø. (h):ø is the 'zero' variant, and indicates the absence of the glottal fricative at the beginning of words like *hotel* and *honey.* Phonetic and phonological variables in the literature are regularly represented in this way; we will extend this use to lexical and grammatical variables too. When representing a list of variants, each variant will be separated by '~'. For instance, if we wanted to represent four different words denoting the meaning 'very good' in current British English, we would represent this as ('very good'): *sound ~ grand ~ mint ~ boss,* etc.

The linguistic variable is fundamental to the study of social variation – Chambers (2003: 26) described the linguistic variable as a "momentous innovation" in linguistic inquiry – so we need to establish why it is considered to be so important. First, as noted above, it tells us something about what speakers know about language – the linguistic variable is part of a speaker's linguistic system. But there may be some motivation for a speaker to select from the range of variants, and sociolinguistic studies have shown that the variables correlate with a number of other parameters, of which some of the main ones are: the social characteristics of the speaker (their ethnic group membership, for instance); the nature of the discourse, or speech style (the extent to which the discourse is formal); the audience (whether the speaker is talking to an intimate friend or a stranger, for instance); and the linguistic context in which the variable appears. This last is critical. Linguistic constraints can affect very significantly the likelihood of a particular variant being selected; in fact, linguistic constraints are often more significant in establishing patterns of variation than social constraints are. For instance, to return to our example of H-Dropping, (h):[h] is rarely selected – by most speakers of British English, irrespective of their social characteristics, the discourse context and their addressees – if the word in which the variable appears is unstressed. So for instance, in a phrase like *his house*, under normal speech conditions, the first of these words, *his*, receives less prominence (and is therefore considered unstressed) relative to the second word, *house*. Many speakers will pronounce *his* as [ɪz] since the word is unstressed; however, the likelihood of pronouncing *house* as [aʊs], rather than [haʊs], has less to do with the matter of linguistic stress, and more to do with the social and stylistic factors relating to the participants in the discourse, and the discourse itself.

Although phonological, lexical and morphosyntactic variables are all structured in the same way (that is, each variable has a set of variants), it seems as if different kinds of variable may be put to use by speakers in different ways. Some recent studies concerning the geographical diffusion of sound changes have noticed the following general trends:

- Speakers use different sets of sounds to mark identity. In other words, evidence from studies of UK dialects suggests that local identity tends to be marked more clearly by variation in vowels; consonantal variants have a very wide geographic distribution, and so typically do not function as highly localised forms (Williams and Kerswill 1999; but see Watson 2006 for an interesting counterexample to this trend in Liverpool English). For example, in the British Isles, variation in vowels such as those in words like *face* and *price* allow listeners to identify speakers as belonging to a particular regional area much more easily than a phenomenon like H-Dropping or TH-Fronting (as we have seen, in TH-Fronting the dental fricatives [θ] and [ð] are replaced by [f] and [v] respectively).

- When such consonantal variants diffuse regionally, they typically do so from urban areas (typically economic centres) into rural areas, rather than vice versa – see, for example, the development of TH-Fronting as described in Kerswill (2003). Why this has happened is a matter of some debate; one suggestion has been that changing patterns of employment and a willingness to travel over larger distances to commute to work may have some role to play (Trudgill 1986).

- Trudgill (1999a) has suggested that this kind of diffusion may lead to the realignment of traditional rural and geographically more compact varieties into more widespread regions dominated by a particular urban centre.

This realignment of dialect boundaries has a number of consequences for perceptions of Standard English in England. Kerswill (2002) has shown that grammatical and lexical variables on the one hand, and phonetic variables on the other, can diffuse in different ways, and have different social correlates. The spread of grammatical and lexical variables within England has been greatly influenced by the language of the middle classes from the south-east of England, in careful speech styles. It is this kind of spoken language that approximates most closely to the standard variety we discussed in Chapters 1 and 3, such that many parts of England are now very similar in terms of grammatical and lexical features. Certain changes affecting phonetic or accent variables, by contrast, have often not spread beyond the south-east (this is particularly true of variation in vowels, as we will see below). Instead, what we can witness is a series of local norms being negotiated by speakers, and these norms typically centre on urban centres like Newcastle and Manchester. This issue of dialect contact will be considered in more detail in Chapter 8.

A very important part of Kerswill's work, and that of many other specialists who carry out research into accents and dialects of English, is that it brings together the work of traditional dialectologists with the work of urban sociolinguists. In order to understand the specific features of urban sociolinguistics, we need to consider what quantitative studies of variation can tell us about how varieties of English are structured and are used by speakers.

4.5 A first example of quantitative variation in English

We begin with a fairly straightforward example of variation, in order to show how the concept of the linguistic variable is employed in the literature. The data in Figure 4.3 come from a study carried out in Bradford

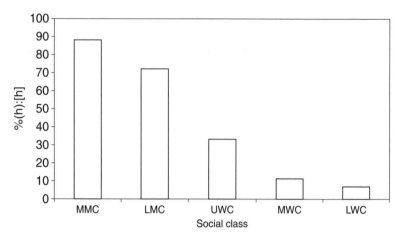

Figure 4.3 (h) in Yorkshire (based on Petyt 1980: 189).

in Yorkshire, England, in the 1970s, and illustrates the correlation of the (h) variable introduced above with a particular social category, namely social class. In this figure, MMC = middle-middle class, LMC = lower-middle class, UWC = upper-working class, MWC = middle-working class and LWC = lower-working class.

The data here illustrate the following:

- Looking at the first and last bars in the chart, we see that at neither end of the class continuum is there exclusive use of one variant. In other words, some speakers in even the highest social class occasionally use (h):ø, while some speakers in even the lowest social class occasionally use (h):[h]. This illustrates a typical pattern of quantitative studies: that most speakers have a knowledge and command of variability, that variation is typical, rather than unusual.
- (h) in Bradford shows clear stratification with social class – the higher the social class, the greater the incidence of (h):[h].
- Unusually for phonetic and phonological variables, (h) sharply stratifies social classes – the biggest drop in the use of (h):[h] occurs between the lower-middle class and the upper-working class. It is normally the case that grammatical variables (such as negation markers) function as sharp stratifiers of social groups, with phonetic and phonological variables offering a more fine-grained set of distinctions.

On the other hand, the data as presented here do not illustrate the following:

- We have no way of knowing – from the data as it is presented here – what the behaviour of individual speakers within each of the social classes was. For instance, it might have been the case that there were some speakers in the lowest social class who were consistently using (h):ø, while others were using (h):ø fairly infrequently. Indeed, as Petyt (1980: 189) points out, at least one individual in each of the two middle-class groups consistently had (h):[h], while at least one individual in each of the three working-class groups consistently had (h):ø. What we are presented with here (and what we are usually presented with in many sociolinguistic surveys) are group scores, and not scores for individuals.
- By isolating social class, it is not possible to see what other social factors may correlate with use of (h). For instance, it is not possible to establish from the data here whether (h) also correlates with the sex of the speaker.
- The data here do not provide information about stylistic variation; we do not know the distribution of (h) in different 'types of talk'.
- No statistical tests are given here to establish whether or not the differences are significant, or whether they are simply down to chance.
- We do not know what the linguistic constraints on the variation might be.

It is important, therefore, to treat all data sets with caution; any claims that are made concerning the relationship between social stratification and linguistic variation need to be supported by particular kinds of evidence, and typically should be shown to be statistically significant.

4.6 The issue of style

As we saw in Section 4.3. above, some sociolinguistic interviews involve speakers engaged in different kinds of linguistic tasks. One motivation for this was because it was thought that speakers pay varying amounts of attention to the actual act of speaking depending on what kind of activity they are involved in. For instance, in relatively informal conversation, it was said that speakers pay lower attention to speech than they do when reading aloud a list of words. The patterns associated with stylistic variation are of great importance in quantitative sociolinguistics, because stylisitic variation intersects with social variation. Sociolinguists have identified three different models associated with stylistic variation: attention to speech, style as audience design and style as speaker design.

Attention to speech was a significant issue in early sociolinguistic accounts of stylistic variation. The hypothesis was that speakers will use a higher proportion of non-local forms when they are speaking formally, or given particular tasks to do which focus their attention on particular aspects of language. For instance, if a speaker is asked to read out a list of words while being interviewed, they may use fewer local forms than they might if they were having a normal conversation, because they are concentrating on a particular (and rather unnatural) linguistic task; and they might use yet fewer forms if they are asked to read out a list of pairs of words which differ only in terms of the linguistic variable under investigation. The results of such studies (see Labov 1972 for some examples) typically showed that all groups of speakers behave in the same way with respect to stylistic variation – each group had a higher proportion of the non-local form in more careful speech styles. Furthermore, there was little to distinguish, in terms of proportions of variants, between the casual speech of the highest social class and the careful speech of the lowest social class.

Although this was quite a well-accepted account of stylistic variation, some researchers began to seek motivations for stylistic variation. One proposal was that speakers display stylistic variation in order to accommodate to a (real or perceived) audience. An important account of this idea of style as 'audience design' comes from a study in New Zealand (Bell 1984), in which a newsreader was recorded reading the same news script for two different radio stations, one whose demographic was largely middle-class, and another whose demographic was largely working-class. Bell found that the newsreader's accent changed depending on which radio station he was reading for. Notice that in this experiment, the only significant difference is the perceived radio audience – the speaker was the same, the speech context and formality were the same, and the script was the same. Yet the newsreader used a higher proportion of (t):[ɾ] variants with the 'working-class' audience, and a higher proportion of (t): [t] variants with the 'middle-class' audience. The announcer was accommodating (changing his behaviour to approximate to his idea of that of others) to the norms of his imagined audience. A study in Cardiff (Coupland 1984) displayed similar results. Here a travel agent was recorded speaking to a number of different clients (from different social classes), and again the agent used more non-local forms with customers from higher social classes, and more local forms with customers from lower social classes. A particularly interesting finding from this study was that the agent used different variables to accommodate to different social groups – so some variables worked as 'middle-class accommodators' and others as 'working-class accommodators'. This shows how finely tuned our knowledge of variation may be, and how specific language users are in accommodating to others.

In contrast, the notion of style as speaker design is concerned again with the issue of identity, and with a more agentive approach to variation, focusing on the speaker's creativity in displays of speech style. In this model, style is largely a reflection of the kinds of linguistic resources a speaker has, which she can use to create and index a set of social relations. This more performative view of style suggests that speakers are constantly restructuring the social space in which they operate. Since style is essentially a marker of intra-speaker variation, we can associate stylistic variation with some of the ways a speaker positions himself in relation to a perceived social space, to index the kind of social relations he understands to exist between him and other individuals. We will return to the notion of speaker agency when we consider third-wave approaches to variation in the following section, which explores how more general theories of sociolinguistics have evolved. This provides a summary of how thinking about social variation (in English, and in other languages) has developed, as well as reflecting some changes in methodology.

4.7 The three waves of variationist sociolinguistics

Some sociolinguists (for example, Eckert 2005) have considered the evolution of the discipline as consisting of three waves, which can be characterised by the methodology adopted and the research objectives. The first wave (associated with variationist studies in the 1960s and 1970s, such as Labov 1966 and Trudgill 1974) was concerned with surveys of urban populations, where informants were selected using a method of (quasi-)random sampling. Many such surveys were concerned with the relationship between variation and ongoing change in the community (see Chapter 5), particularly with the social embedding and transmission of language change. The second wave of studies, exemplified by Rickford (1986), took a broadly ethnographic approach: investigators spent a great deal of time in the community under observation, becoming part of that community in some cases, and trying to understand the social practices of the individuals involved. While the community under investigation was typically much smaller than that in the first wave studies, the period of time spent observing the informants was much greater. Such studies began to consider the social meaning of linguistic variation, and the projection of identity which could be shown to correlate with particular linguistic practices. The studies also aimed to show connections between local and supra-local linguistic patterns. The issue of identity has become even more prominent in the third wave of social dialectology, where variation (particularly stylistic variation) was associated with social practice. Each of these 'waves' is discussed below. The first wave identified by Eckert (2005) typically involved gross social categorisation of the community under investigation. One of the problems associated with the association of linguistic variation with such gross social categorisation is that the social categories employed were often conceived of as being rather inflexible, and understood as being predominantly 'labels', rather than 'ways of being'. For instance, early sociolinguistic analyses of linguistic differences in the speech of men and women were often interpreted as binary sex differences (male vs. female) rather than gradient gender differences (clines of masculinity and femininity associated with gender roles in different communities). A nice example of how a social category is gradient rather than binary is provided by the following observation, from the *Observer Magazine* (Sunday 16 July 2006, p. 8). These are the words of a Los Angeles tattoo artist named Zulu, discussing a change, during his childhood, in his attitude to being black: "After that, not wanting to be black went away. After that, I wanted to be as black as I could get." Being black is not simply an issue of skin colour; it can also be part of an individual's identity. Recognising this allows us to understand why some white speakers adopt linguistic practices associated primarily with black speakers: using language associated typically with a particular social group is a way of projecting an identity, showing solidarity and promoting affinity with one group, while simultaneously marking 'difference' with another. Such acts of identity (Le Page and Tabouret-Keller 1985) are critical for our understanding of linguistic variation in English, and were sometimes overlooked by some of the earlier quantitative sociolinguistic studies.

The second wave approach typically involves social networks of the kind discussed in Chapter 2. Social network approaches to variation in English are probably best known through the work of James and Lesley Milroy in Belfast in the 1970s, though other studies that both pre- and post-date the Milroys' work have used the concept of a social network. A network approach is typically more centred on individual behaviours and patterns than on those of larger groups. This is not to say that group patterns are irrelevant; but what is foregrounded is the social ties that bind a set of individuals, and the linguistic patterns that can be shown to be correlated with the number and nature of those ties. Social networks have been used to explain the persistence of local variants in situations of dialect contact. In the Belfast studies mentioned above, the strength of the social network correlated in many instances with the use of particular linguistic forms: local variants (such as the deletion of the intervocalic consonant [ð] in words like *father* and *brother*) were found most frequently in strong (that is, more dense and more multiplex) networks, while supra-local variants were favoured by those whose networks were typically weak. Network structure was not the only social variable to be considered in these studies – gender too played an important role in the variation; more importantly, gender and network interacted in the social make-up of the various working-class communities that were investigated in Belfast. Often, disruption to traditional employment patterns meant that either men had to find work beyond their local community, or women had to go out and find work, or both. This led to disruption in the fabric of the social network, which may have facilitated the spread of innovations into the local accent.

Third wave studies are also concerned with local practices, and have often been linked to the community of practice, also discussed in Chapter 2. Such studies are particularly concerned with the social meaning of variation in a given community, and place a very strong emphasis on the kind of stylistic variation discussed in Section 4.6 above. Third wave approaches require the analyst to look closely at local features of variation that cannot be recovered by gross social categorisation. For instance, (t) in final position has been shown to mark a number of identities in different communities of practice in the United States; the variation itself has a meaning, and these meanings are layered, just as groups in a community may be layered. For instance, for many American speakers, the full release variant of (t) in final position in a word (for example, [bɪt] for *bit*) has connotations of 'Britishness' (Eckert 2005). But in particular communities, release of final (t) may be associated with being an intelligent, 'bookish' female (Bucholtz 1998) or with fussiness and preciseness among some gay men (Podesva et al. 2002). Clearly issues of stereotyping and inferencing are relevant here (for example, 'British' may imply 'intelligent', and 'intelligent' may imply 'geek'; or 'British' may imply 'precise', and 'precise' imply 'fussy'), but these are not generalisations we can apply to every community. These patterns of variation – and the meanings associated with the variation – are connected, but may be highly localised, and suggest a very fine-grained correlation between patterns of variation and social meaning.

Third wave sociolinguistic studies show that the study of variation in English has developed quite substantially since the days of the *Survey of English Dialects*. But the final section of this chapter looks at some of the ways in which regional and social variation may be synthesised in a rather different way.

4.8 Synthesising regional and social variation

An important development in the study of varieties of English is the bringing together of work on regional and social dialectology by considering geographical space as a kind of social category. In the sections above, we looked at the way in which various dimensions of social categories are constructed and negotiated by speakers, partly through language. In other words, ethnicity or gender, for example, is not something you are, but something you do. If this is true of categories like gender and ethnic group membership, is it also true for your sense of place: is 'Cockney' or 'New Yorker' something you are, or something you do? In other words, your regional group membership is yet another aspect of your identity which might be reflected – and constructed – by various linguistic practices.

In Middlesbrough, in the north-east of England, research has been carried out to look at how speakers orient themselves with respect to competing claims on local identity. Recent research in the area explored the way in which different groups of speakers negotiated their identity in part by the linguistic forms they used, and considered how the use of particular forms correlated with overt comments on regional identity which the informants expressed. Llamas (2007) studied the distribution of glottalised variants of the voiceless stop variables (p), (t) and (k), and found that phonetic patterns associated with the largest conurbation in the area (Newcastle, some 40 miles to the north) were typically being used by younger females, distinguishing them not only from older speakers, but also from more southerly pronunciations in Yorkshire. (Middlesbrough was officially part of a Yorkshire local government area until 1968.) Llamas also found that younger speakers were more likely to identify themselves as north-easterners, as opposed to the older speakers, who saw themselves more as coming from Yorkshire. However, the young people also did not see themselves as 'Geordies' (the name given to people who come from Newcastle): they saw themselves as distinct. Llamas has argued that her research on Middlesbrough English has suggested that place is not an objective given; rather that the "psychological reality of place is not fixed . . . but is socially constructed and can shift" (Llamas 2007: 582).

This research supports the claims made by Britain (2002) that research into linguistic variation need consider space in a number of ways:

- Euclidean space (which is objective and asocial);
- social space (how humans use geographical areas for particular communal activities, including the political organisation of geographic areas);

- perceived space (how, in the practice of particular activities, beliefs about space evolve and can be shared across communities).

Taken together, these constitute spatiality (Britain 2002: 604), and it is this coming together of Euclidean, social and perceived space that can give rise to the kind of dialect isoglosses we identified earlier. We will return to this notion of spatiality when we consider patterns of dialect contact in Chapter 8.

4.9 Summary

Contemporary studies of varieties of English are now typically both regional and social. Partly this is to do with the various social factors that are shaping new regional dialects; but as we shall see in Chapter 6, when we look at English historical sociolinguistics, we will see that English accents and dialects have always had regional and social bases. What we see in many new regional varieties of English is the product of particular social, political and economic developments in particular communities; so in studying varieties of English, it is important to 'think practically and look locally' (Eckert and McConnell-Ginet 1992b). For example, the new regional varieties of English in England are no longer characterised by the traditional rural or the traditional working-class urban varieties; however, not all vestiges of local forms have disappeared, so in accent at least, we cannot talk of a national standard. What we witness is the creation of new, non-local, non-standard forms, which is a matter of language change, the topic of the next chapter.

Exercises

1. This exercise is about regional variation, and particularly, about dialect words. How many different words do you use to refer to the following concepts? Example: for the concept 'mother', I use the words *mother* (rarely) and *mam* (frequently).
   - (a) 'carbonated beverage'
   - (b) 'female sibling'
   - (c) 'bad tempered'
   - (d) 'the smallest finger on your hand'
   - (e) 'the nicest room in the house, where you would normally host visitors'

2. This exercise is about social variation, and particularly about accent. Think of an accent feature which you consider to be a clear stereotype,

either of your own local accent, or of another accent of English which you are familiar with. With what kind of speaker would you associate that pronunciation? Would you expect to find it in all speech styles? How would you design an experiment to work out whether this stereotype is still a feature of the accent, or whether it is just an archaism which is no longer actively used?

Further reading

Some excellent electronic resources for regional variation in English are now available, such as Labov et al. (2005) and the Kortmann et al. (2004) handbook. Regional variation in English is covered by a number of texts, including Wells (1982), Foulkes and Docherty (1999), Beal (2006) and Britain (2007). Many books on sociolinguistics have a lot of data on English (see the list of references in the introduction), as does Chambers et al. (2002). More general work on regional and social dialectology is discussed in Chambers and Trudgill (1998). For work on stylistic variation, see Schilling-Estes (2002) and Coupland (2007).

5 Change in English

5.1 Overview

In Chapter 4 we saw how sociolinguistic research has proven that linguistic variation is not random, but structured, and that such research provides a methodology for the systematic study of the linguistic behaviour of individuals in networks and communities of various kinds. In other words, sociolinguistics can help us understand some of the ways in which varieties of English (whether those varieties are associated with individuals or with groups of individuals) display the patterns that they do. In this chapter, we consider the relationship between this patterned variation and processes of linguistic change in English. In particular, we will consider whether sociolinguistics can tell us anything about changes which are ongoing.

5.2 What is linguistic change?

We saw in previous chapters that many researchers see English as varying in two ways – regionally (or diatopically) and socially, that is, in terms of the social characteristics and practices of individuals and communities who speak English. But English has also varied in another way. Consider examples (1) to (3) below, which are all recipes taken from different periods of English: Middle English, early Modern English and present-day English. The first two examples come from the British Library's website *Books for Cooks* (http://www.bl.uk/learning/langlit/booksforcooks/booksforcooks.html).

> (1) Take Capouns and seeþ hem, þenne take hem up. take Almandes blaunched. grynd hem and alay hem up with the same broth. cast the mylk in a pot. waisshe rys and do þerto and lat it seeþ.
> (Blanc Mang, from *The Forme of Cury*, c.1390)
> (2) Take a pint and somewhat more of thick Cream, ten Eggs, put the

whites of three, beat them very well with two spoonfuls of Rose-water: mingle with your Cream three spoonfuls of fine flower: mingle it so well, that there be no lumps in it, put it altogether, and season it according to your Tast.

(Quaking Pudding, from *The Queens Closet Opened*, 1665)

(3) While the chillies are steaming, gently rip up your mozzarella into 4 or 5 pieces and randomly place on a large plate. Peel and deseed the chillies and slice lengthways as thinly as you like. It's quite important to scatter them evenly over the mozzarella and very important to wash your hands after doing so before you rub your eyes or anything else! Now rip up some purple and green basil over the top, and sprinkle with sea salt and freshly ground black pepper. Add a little squeeze of lemon juice and a generous lug of olive oil. Nice one.

(Mozzarella and grilled chilli salad, from Oliver 2000: 56)

Diachronic variation is variation over time: English in the twenty-first century has a different shape from that in the fourteenth century. But there is also some continuity – we can see similarities in these texts from the same genre despite the fact that they were written in different periods. Here are some of the ways in which the Englishes in (1) to (3) are similar to and different from each other:

Similarities:

- Since the texts are all from the same genre, we might expect to see some general similarities in the kind of language used. For instance, notice that many of the clauses in the texts have the form of imperatives (for example, *Peel and deseed the chillies*), since the function of the text is to direct the reader in a certain course of action (namely preparing food).

- In the second and third text, there is a distinctive use of the second person possessive pronoun (*your*) in *mingle with your Cream* (text 2) and *gently rip up your mozzarella* (text 3). In instructional discourse, this seems to be a variant to mark general definiteness rather than specific possession, in that it seems to have the same meaning as *the* (rather than, say, contrasting with other possessive determiners like *his* or *my*).

Differences:

- Orthographic change: the letter shape <þ> (known as 'thorn', from the runic alphabet) is no longer used in English, having been replaced by the digraph <th>. So <seeþ> in text 1 is a Middle English spelling of *seethe*.

- Morphological change: the third person plural object pronoun *hem* has been replaced by *them*. These *th*-pronoun forms are the result of long-term contact in northern England between English and Old Norse in the Middle English period (see Chapter 6).

- Semantic/syntactic change: the verb *seethe* in Middle English could be used transitively (since it can take a direct object): *seeþ hem*, literally 'seethe them'. But in Modern English, the meaning of the word has changed (from 'boil' to 'be angry'), and this has had consequences for its syntactic behaviour – it is now only used intransitively, and usually collocates with the prepositional phrase *with rage*.

- Lexical change: new words have entered the language (*chilli*, *mozzarella*).

- Stylistic or textual change: the first text consists solely of imperative clauses, functioning as directives, and the impression created for a modern reader is of an impersonal, purely instructive text. The final text, however, has a mixture of clause types: for instance, it includes a declarative clause, beginning *It's quite important*. The function of the clause is still a directive (the author is still instructing readers to scatter the chillies in a particular way, and to wash their hands), but its grammatical form is different. Along with the phrase *Nice one*, which acts as a solidarity and politeness marker, this variation creates a text which is equally instructive, but seems to reduce the social distance between the author and the reader.

Even from such brief examples as these, we can see that English has changed in many ways: its writing system, its spelling (and associated pronunciations), its grammar and its lexical stock. But in order for us to provide a systematic examination of such changes, we need recourse to more systematically collected data. Our next question must therefore be this: how did such changes come about? Sociolinguists have provided a great deal of evidence to suggest that linguistic change – change in the structure of a particular variety – materialises when the linguistic system is employed by speakers for communicative purposes, in a particular social context. Systemic changes in English emerge from language use and social practices.

5.3 An example of variation in the past

The texts in (4) below are examples of early Modern English. Examples (4a) and (4b) are from Shakespeare's *King Lear*, written at the start of the seventeenth century, and (4c) and (4d) are from mid-seventeenth-century court records and depositions.

(4a) He **hath** been out nine years, and away he shall again. The king is coming. (Shakespeare, *King Lear* I, i, 31–2)

(4b)   What **says** our second daughter
Our dearest Regan, wife of Cornwall?
(Shakespeare, *King Lear*, I, i, 6–7)

(4c) The informant **saith**, that two Monthes since or thereabouts going along ffishers streete in the towne of Barking vpon his occasions (from an account given to Essex Justices of the Peace, 28 June 1645, in Cusack 1998: 33)

(4d) And further **saith** that he **hath** heard Goody Penny (who **lives** neere the said Ward) say about that tyme that (from the deposition of Stephen Badcocke taken in Essex in 1645, in Cusack 1998: 146).

Notice the variation in the inflectional suffix which marks present tense on verbs whose subjects are third person singular (such words are emboldened in the examples in (4) above): sometimes it is spelt with -*th*, sometimes with -*s*. By the time we get to contemporary English, something has changed: one morphological form (the -*s* form) has ousted another (the -*th* form). In the early modern period, both variants were well attested; now, only the -*s* form has survived. This illustrates a critical issue for the sociolinguistic study of language change: all change must have its origin in variation.

What kinds of questions can we ask about the progression of a linguistic change? In a landmark paper on the topic, Weinreich et al. (1968) identified the following problems:

- Constraints: what constraints exist on possible changes (including those specifically in a given language at a given time)?
- Actuation: why does a change begin in a language at time t1, and not at time t2? Why does the change begin in variety v1 but not in variety v2?
- Transition: how does a change develop, from stage s1 to stage s2, or from form f1 to form f2?
- Embedding: how is the change embedded in both the linguistic system and the community in which the language is spoken?
- Evaluation: how do speakers in the community evaluate the change? Are they aware of the change? Has f1 or f2 become stigmatised?

These questions can be applied directly to an example of a sound change in some varieties of British English, the loss of /r/ in words like *far* and *farm*.

- Constraints: the loss of /r/ in particular places in a word helps us to understand what is a possible (and what is an impossible) phonological change.

- Actuation: why is the systematic loss of /r/ first recorded in the eighteenth century, but not in the twelfth or sixteenth century? Why is /r/-loss common in most varieties of British English but not in (say) most varieties of North American English?

- Transition: does the /r/ just disappear from one generation to the next, or is there some intermediate development?

- Embedding: where and among which social groups is /r/-loss first recorded? What is its current distribution in the community under investigation? What is the influence of the phonological environment?

- Evaluation: what kind of a sociolinguistic variable is (r) in a particular community? Is /r/-loss stigmatised?

While all change must have its origin in variation, not all variation implies change. Sociolinguistic studies of English (and other languages) have shown that certain variables may correlate with social and/or stylistic categories for speakers and/or types of discourse, but there is no evidence of a linguistic change taking place: in other words, there is simply stable sociolinguistic variation. We can make a further distinction between innovation (in an idiolect) and change (which involves spread), on which see further Milroy (1992), and note that while an innovation will certainly mean an increase (however trivial) in variation, it will not necessarily lead to a change. How then are we to distinguish between stable sociolinguistic variation and ongoing language change?

5.4 The linguistic behaviour of older and younger speakers in a community

One piece of evidence which we can use to figure out whether a particular linguistic change is in progress among a group of speakers is to look at differences between older and younger members of that group. In other words, age is the critical speaker variable in situations of language change. Figure 5.1 shows age-related differences in the use of a phonological variable in Canadian English, (hw), with variants (hw): [w] and (hw):[ʍ], the latter of which is the conservative variant.

Looking at the distribution of variants for the oldest speakers in the sample, we can see that while both (hw):[w] and (hw):[ʍ] are used by members of this particular subgroup, (hw):[ʍ] is the preferred variant for older speakers; by contrast, when we look at the youngest

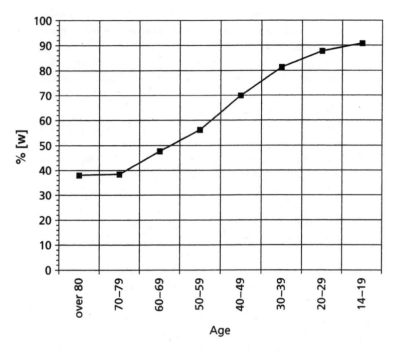

Figure 5.1 Percentage of (hw):[w] in central Canada by age (Chambers 2002: 360).

speakers, (hw):[w] is preferred. This therefore appears to be an example of change: the variant favoured by the older speakers is being displaced by a variant favoured by younger speakers. In other words, typically only older speakers in this part of Canada will make a distinction between *which* and *witch*, or *whales* and *Wales* – when younger Canadians talk, *which* and *witch* typically sound identical.

But how do we really know this is an example of change? Could it not be the case that the oldest group of speakers are using (hw):[ʍ] more frequently now, but used (hw):[w] more frequently when they were in their twenties? We can answer this question by considering two things: the apparent-time hypothesis and real-time data.

The apparent-time hypothesis is as follows. Assuming that other factors (social and stylistic variables, for instance) are kept constant, differences in the use of particular variants by different age groups are a reflection of diachronic linguistic changes within that community: "people of different ages preserve the speech patterns of their formative years. Speech differences between people of different ages therefore reflect differences in the way people spoke in those years" (Chambers 2002: 358). The hypothesis makes the claim that the speech of a 40-year-old today is the same as that of a 20-year-old twenty years ago; so if we compare the language of a group of speakers aged 40 and a group of speakers aged 20, any differences which appear may be evidence of a linguistic change in progress.

Researchers can supplement these data – and thereby provide evidence to support the apparent-time hypothesis – by making use of whatever real-time data are available to them. Real-time data come in a number of forms. One source of data is a previous record of linguistic variation in the community under observation, like the *Dictionary of American Regional English* (Cassidy and Hall 1985–2002) or the Origins of New Zealand English (ONZE) corpus (see Gordon et al. 2004). This is not without problems. First, there is the issue of the speaker sample. As we saw in Chapter 4, the methods of the traditional dialectologists and those of variationist sociolinguists can be radically different, so that the kind of speaker used in each survey – and therefore the kind of speech recorded – may not be consistent, and the researchers using both data sets to compare apparent-time and real-time data may not be comparing like with like. Second, the way the data were recorded is variable: earlier dialectological surveys did not necessarily use tape-recorders (so there is no means of verifying the transcription), and the transcription methods used by earlier dialectologists may not be the same as those used by sociolinguists. However, some earlier tape recordings may be available, which may facilitate more detailed transcriptions.

In order to avoid such problems, researchers have devised other methods of accessing real-time data. One example of this is a survey carried out by Mees and Collins (1999), who were investigating variation in Cardiff English. Rather than using pre-existing data collected by an earlier group of researchers, Mees and Collins attempted to interview the same group of speakers at different times (in 1976, when the informants were aged between 9 and 11, in 1981 and in 1990). Their survey provided some real-time evidence to suggest that the incidence of T-Glottaling (the replacement of [t] with [ʔ], typically in intervocalic or final position) was on the increase in Cardiff English in the latter part of the twentieth century; the survey also suggested that the change was being led by young middle-class females. Surveys such as this provide excellent real-time evidence of changes, but are not without their own problems: for instance, no results can be published for a considerable period of time, since it is necessary to collect data over a long time span, and not all of the informants will necessarily be willing or able to be recorded at successive intervals, as Mees and Collins discovered: of the eighty informants they used in 1976, seventy-five were re-recorded in 1981, and that figure fell to fifty-four in 1990. This kind of panel study (where the same speakers are re-interviewed at different points in time) contrasts with a trend study (where different but comparable speakers from the community are interviewed).

A further issue relating to language and age is that of age-grading, whereby speakers may change their linguistic behaviour during their lifetime. There is some evidence that speakers, particularly those who are regularly exposed to standard varieties in their daily lives, may use a higher proportion of standard variants in their 'middle years', but use a higher proportion of vernacular variants in their youth, and in old age. Age-grading, therefore, is an idiolectal change across a lifespan, but not a linguistic change across generations.

Finally, it is the case that not all types of linguistic variable change in the same way. For instance, with a lexical variable, you have a discrete choice between one variant and another (for example, *couch* or *chesterfield* or *sofa*, etc.), but with phonetic variants, the choices may be more gradient. For example, if a sound change is ongoing whereby a low vowel like [ɑ] is being fronted to [a], it may be that the sound is changing via incrementation (Labov 2007); if it is gradually moving from back to front along a phonetic cline, rather than a 'leap' directly to [a] from [ɑ], a child acquiring a language may observe that other speakers have a more 'fronted' vowel, and so develop the change further by fronting the vowel even more frequently. A sound change which develops in a gradual way phonetically, but which simultaneously affects all the words that have the sound undergoing change, is known as a Neogrammarian change (named after a group of linguists in nineteenth-century Europe, the Neogrammarians, who pioneered the study of sound change) – such changes are phonetically gradual, but lexically abrupt; a sound change which involves a discrete phonetic change, but which affects some words in the set before others, is known as a lexically diffusing change – such changes are phonetically abrupt, but lexically gradual.

5.5 Other social factors in change

Given the fact that change involves variation over time, it is clear that any analysis of linguistic change will need to take age as the primary non-linguistic correlate. None the less, there are other patterns which can be observed in sociolinguistic variation that serve as indicators of linguistic change in progress. We will make use of the first, second and third wave distinction introduced in Chapter 4 to structure this part of the discussion.

First wave sociolinguistic investigations into change (for example, Labov 1966) identified two different kinds of linguistic change, change from above and change from below (see also Labov 1994). 'Above' and 'below' refer simultaneously to two different but related levels: a level of group social status, and a level of individual consciousness. Changes from above are typically introduced into a speech community through dialect contact (see Chapter 8), and appear first in the careful, formal speech of a high-status social class (though not always the highest social class). Often such changes have subsequent effects elsewhere in the linguistic system (for example, the reintroduction of /r/ in words like *far* and *farm* in New York, discussed by Labov (1966), promoted some further changes in the vowel sounds which precede the /r/ in such words). Changes from below represent more general changes which are not (at least initially) driven by social forces, because they may appear first in the casual speech of any social class. Often these changes may correlate with patterns of local identity.

In the earliest sociolinguistic studies, particularly those which involved class stratification, one regularly occurring pattern which was shown to be indicative of a particular kind of linguistic change was hypercorrection. Hypercorrection concerns the interplay of social and stylistic variation, and is typically used to describe the linguistic behaviour of middle-status groups in more formal speech styles. Such speakers have been observed to use a higher proportion of standard variants in such styles than speakers in the social class above them did. This shows up in graphic form as a crossover pattern in more formal speech styles, and this irregular pattern of class and style stratification is taken as a sign of linguistic change in progress. Reasons which have been suggested for this hypercorrect behaviour of the middle-status groups include the social insecurity and higher social aspirations associated with those speakers.

First wave studies are also concerned with the role of factors like speaker sex and ethnic group membership in the propagation of changes. In terms of sex and gender, for instance, Labov (1990) attempted to summarise the linguistic behaviour of men and women in relation to language variation and change in terms of a set of principles:

- Principle I: In cases of stable sociolinguistic variation, women use standard variants more frequently than men do (assuming that other variables such as style remain constant).
- Principle Ia: In cases of change from above, women use the incoming prestige variant more frequently than men do.

- Principle II: In cases of change from below, women are usually the innovators (though there are some significant exceptions to this, where men have been in the vanguard of change).

As a result, then, we may wish to consider more generally how changes spread through a community. Labov (1994: 300–1) points out how a number of factors may be involved, basing his claims on a series of studies of vowel shifts in contemporary American English. Leaders in linguistic change tend to be younger women at the mid-point of the class hierarchy (that is, in the upper-working class, typically), who are held in high esteem at a local level (perhaps because of the job they do, or the ethnic group to which they belong). Notice that when a variant is new in a community, it may not carry significant social meaning, which may go some way to explain the apparent contradiction in the principles listed above. Some women may abandon innovations only when they become loaded with social meaning (for example, by becoming a feature of a low-status group with which the speakers do not wish to be associated). The linguistic change establishes itself as a group marker, and as it generalises, it becomes recognised as such by those not part of the group. It is at this point that the change comes to have a particular 'value' associated with it (by virtue of being a group marker); as the change develops, that value may be renegotiated by those in adjacent social groups. The variation may become more salient as more and more speakers subconsciously evaluate the variants, with the old variant associated with one set of values, and the new variant associated with a different set. If the change continues to be subconsciously evaluated, the variable may acquire stylistic properties, and become a marker. (Variables that are not subject to stylistic variation, only to social variation, are known as indicators.) If the change is subject to overt comment (and possible criticism), the change may become more limited, and the variable develops as a stereotype. (See Labov 1994: 78 for more on markers, indicators and stereotypes.)

Changes go to completion when the older variants become associated solely with older speakers, and disappear, or become part of fixed phrases (for example, in the case of the variation described in (4), the -th variant is no longer productive, and only appears in idioms and proverbs of the kind *Hell hath no fury like a woman scorned*).

So far, we have discussed some processes involved in change; but we can discover much about change when we also consider why certain linguistic features are resistant to change. Second wave studies have revealed some interesting patterns regarding resistance to linguistic change. We have seen in Chapter 3 that standard varieties of English, problematic though they are to define formally, are associated with a particular kind of prestige. They are used in domains that are often seen as socially, economically, or politically powerful – in schools, as a medium of government, in print media, and so on. While this is especially true of the written standard, it is also true of the spoken standard. Given that this is the case, it is perhaps surprising to see non-standard varieties of English thriving. This is true not only of non-standard varieties of inner-circle Englishes, using the categorisation proposed by Kachru (1985), such as American English and British English, but also of outer-circle and expanding-circle Englishes such as Singaporean English. Why and how are such varieties continuing to thrive in the face of the pressures and attractions of the standard variety?

Again, we need to return to the speakers, their practices and the social networks within which speakers operate. We saw in Chapters 2 and 4 that sociolinguists like James and Lesley Milroy (Milroy 1992; Milroy 2002) have used the concept of a social network in order to explain linguistic variation within what appears to be a socially homogeneous group, and that such networks vary in terms of their density and plexity (recall the discussion of dense and multiplex networks in Section 2.3 above). Strong networks (often found in working-class and upper-class communities) were those which were relatively dense and multiplex; weak networks (typically found in middle-class communities) were those which were relatively sparse and uniplex. Critically, members of strong networks are less socially and geographically mobile than members of weaker networks. Those in strong networks are more likely to engage in local, neighbourhood-based activities (in terms of employment and socialisation) than those in weak networks; members of a strong, territorially based network interact with each other on a regular basis, and can foster a strong sense of local solidarity. This means that strong networks are resistant to change (both social change and linguistic change), and that speakers who are members of that network are likely to resist the adoption of standard variants. Strong networks are effective local norm-enforcement mechanisms, and deviation from the local norms carries a social risk – therefore, members of such networks who use 'outgroup' standard variants (despite the supra-local power which standard speech might symbolise) are in danger of signalling their own 'outgroup' status through speech.

By contrast, those at the periphery of such networks – speakers who form weak links which function as bridges between strong networks, or who contract only weak networks themselves, or both – are not subject to the same degree of local norm enforcement. This can have a number of repercussions. First, the social and geographical mobility of such speakers means they are more likely to come into contact with a wider range of linguistic varieties. We will explore the consequences of such extensive contact in more detail in Chapters 7 and 8; the critical issue here is that members of weaker networks are more susceptible to the influence of standardising and supra-local varieties because they are more regularly exposed to such varieties, and perhaps identify more with the symbolic values associated with the standard language. Second, the fact that such speakers can function as weak links between strong networks means that the symbolic link of any innovation can itself be weakened by association with these intermediaries. In other words, we can see an overlap between the second and third wave studies in the intersection of social networks and communities of practice in instances of linguistic change.

This can be illustrated by a study of the linguistic behaviour of adolescents in a Detroit suburb (Eckert 1988, 1989, 2000). As a result of long-term participant observation, Eckert was able to identify three main groups of students in high schools in suburban Detroit. Two of these groups – the Jocks and the Burnouts – formed networks which were largely dense and multiplex, although each network was organised differently. The Jock network – comprised of students who were centred on school activities, and who supported the general ethos of the school – was hierarchical; the Burnout network – comprised of students whose interests led them to develop greater links with urban Detroit, and who rejected the school ethos – was largely egalitarian. But in both cases, the groups were tightly knit. The third group of students, however, were more loosely connected with both groups. These 'In-betweens' engaged in some school-based practices associated with the Jocks, and also with some of the urban-based practices associated with the Burnouts.

Eckert not only observed the social practices of these groups (for instance, how they dressed, and how they spent their leisure time), but also analysed their linguistic behaviour, particularly in terms of the groups' participation in a series of related sound changes known as the Northern Cities Shift (NCS; see Labov 1994; Gordon 2002). The NCS is associated with a number of urban centres (for instance Chicago, Detroit and Buffalo) in the northern part of the United States, and is an example of a particular kind of phonological change, known as a vowel rotation, a series of changes to the pronunciation of a set of vowels. For instance, the lowering of /ɪ/ to /ɛ/ means that innovative pronunciations of *bid* sound like conservative pronunciations of *bed*; the backing of /ɛ/ to /ʌ/ means that innovative pronunciations of *bed* sound like conservative pronunciations of *bud*; and so on. While Eckert's study investigates most of these sound changes, we will focus on just one, variation in the *bud* vowel, usually designated (uh). In fact, the linguistic process

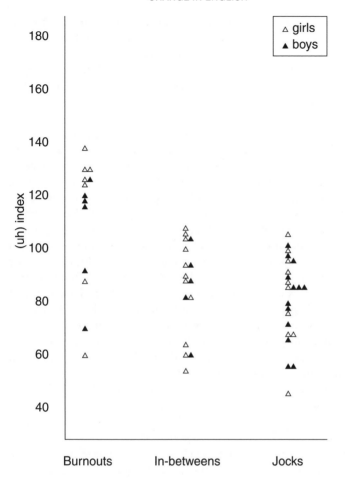

Figure 5.2 Variation in (uh) among Detroit adolescent groups (Eckert 1988: 200).

involved is rather complex: /ʌ/ undergoes not just backing but lowering, and in some lexical items even raising and rounding (see Gordon 2002). So we have (uh): [ʌ] ~ [ɔ] ~ [ʊ] ~ [ɑ], with the first of these being the conservative variant, and the remainder innovations, the last of which is rarer than any of the others. Figure 5.2[1] illustrates the correlation between the index score for (uh) and group membership.

We can observe the following from this figure:

- All groups show variation in (uh), ranging from more conservative to more innovative.

- Despite this significant individual variation within the groups, it is clear that the Burnouts are more innovative than the Jocks. The In-betweens are (perhaps unsurprisingly) in between.

- Cross-cutting this group-based variation is sex-based variation: as discussed above, the female students were generally more innovative than the males.

How are we to interpret these data? First, we need to explain why the Burnouts are leading the change. There has been a range of sociolinguistic studies which have suggested that changes originate in urban centres and spread outwards (see for example Kerswill 2003), so we would expect the group with the greatest contact with urban speakers to be more likely to be in the vanguard of change; given the Burnouts' observed socialisation with inner-city speakers, we can therefore account for the Burnouts leading the change in this suburban adolescent community. Second, we need to explain the Jocks' linguistic behaviour: given that the Jocks are the polar opposites of the Burnouts in terms of their social practices, why should the Jocks be adopting a variant which appears to have a symbolic 'Burnout' value? The answer to this question lies with the In-betweens, who renegotiate the value of the innovation, diluting its symbolic 'Burnout-ness', and making it more acceptable as a variant for the Jocks to adopt. The In-betweens function as weak links between two strong networks – they help to transmit the change from one adolescent community to another.

5.6 Beyond the urban west

Most variationist studies of ongoing change in varieties of English have concentrated on urban communities in the industrialised west. The remainder of this chapter considers changes in English accents and dialects spoken by people living in quite different communities: a rural community in Scotland, and a community living on an island in the Atlantic Ocean.

Huntly is a community in north-eastern Scotland, and research in that area (Marshall 2005) has suggested that many linguistic changes in non-urban centres are exocentric, or brought about by contact, rather than endocentric (or internally motivated) changes, which are characteristic of cities. This has a number of consequences for the kind of variants that are adopted by those driving the change in rural communities. For instance, since rural communities are typically said to be more non-standard than urban centres, rural adolescents who innovate may adopt more standard variants than those used by their elders in the rural community.

Marshall's study showed that the typical pattern among young people in Huntly was a reduction in the use of the local variants. Thus traditional forms such as [hem] and [meːr] for *home* and *more* were increasingly disfavoured by successive generations, in a uniform way. However, with T-Glottaling – (t):[ʔ] in words like *butter* and *cut*, an innovative variant in the Huntly community – the youngest males and females in the sample, aged between 8 and 12, were showing a higher incidence of the local form (t):[t] than the older adolescents were. So two main questions emerged: why did the youngest children (and particularly the youngest girls) have such a low incidence of T-Glottaling? And why did the older adolescents have a relatively high incidence of T-Glottaling?

The answer to the first question lies in an understanding of speaker styles, and the methodology used to collect the data in Huntly. Marshall's study elicited relatively careful speech, and therefore it is possible that even the youngest children were aware that T-Glottaling was somehow 'inappropriate' in more formal, careful talk. But such self-monitoring does not provide an answer to the second question, since with the older adolescents, we have a high incidence of glottal replacement, despite the fact that the elicitation method was consistent across the study. One possible answer to this question relates to the way in which speakers use variants to project and create identities, as discussed in Section 5.5, and in Chapter 4: these data provide some answers to Eckert's question 'How do variables mean?' One of the ways in which the T-Glottaling variable may mean to these older adolescents is that it allows the opportunity of selecting a non-standard, yet non-local, form, introducing a new variant into the local community which conforms neither to local norms, nor to 'proper' speech. Given that the (t) variable in Huntly did not stratify either by social class or by sex (at least for the three oldest age groups), only by age, the notion that such a form may serve as a specific identity marker in the community is an interesting one.

We move now from north-eastern Scotland to what is said to be the most remote group of islands on earth, Tristan da Cunha in the south Atlantic ocean, to look at some research which has explored sociolinguistic variation and change in a geographically isolated and socially homogeneous community on an island with fewer than 300 inhabitants (Schreier 2002, 2003). While Schreier's work has covered variation in both accent and dialect, we will focus on one particular grammatical variable, discussed in detail in Schreier (2002). This variable is known as completive *done*, and is exemplified by examples like those in (5):

(5a) They used to get much more . . . two years ago the pensioners done
       got a free gas bottle. (Schreier 2002: 156)

(5b) That's one of the hottest summers we's ever done had. (Schreier 2002: 156)

The use of *done* as a completive aspect marker (that is, to indicate that the process denoted by the verb has already happened) is not unique to Tristan da Cunha; it is found in other varieties including African American English (Green 2002) and Jamaican Creole (Rickford 1977), as well as some earlier varieties of English, giving rise to the question of whether the form was a feature of the language of the original settlers who brought English to different places around the world, whether there was independent parallel development in these new varieties, or whether an older form was supported and renewed by a similar feature in other languages which were part of the contact. Schreier's research on Tristan da Cunha provides interesting details regarding language change in a community which was settled only from the beginning of the nineteenth century, and which was largely isolated following the development of new trade routes after the Panama canal was opened in 1869. This isolation changed after a military outpost was set up in 1942, and after the entire population had to be evacuated to England during the 1960s, following volcanic disturbances on the island. The linguistic variety which has emerged is in fact a product of contact (of American and British varieties, and of other languages including Dutch and Danish, as well as influence from a group of female settlers from St Helena), despite the island's isolation. With regard to completive *done*, Schreier (2002) found that the aspect marking in Tristan da Cunha English was formally distinct from all the possible input varieties, though there seems to be some overlap in terms of semantic function. Particularly, the research shows how complex the linguistic situation is in communities where (historically) there is a great deal of language and dialect contact: although completive *done* was a feature of earlier English, we cannot simply explain the development in Tristan da Cunha as retention of an archaic form – contact with other varieties has clearly influenced its development. We will take up the issues of historical sociolinguistics and contact linguistics in the following three chapters.

5.7 Summary

Quantitative sociolinguistics can tell us a great deal about the mechanisms and motivations of relevance to linguistic change. In addition to the findings of large-scale urban dialectology, which has revealed a great deal about the processes of language change, other studies – which involve detailed ethnographic work in urban communities, and/or analysis of linguistic variation in non-urban areas – enrich our understanding of how varieties of English have evolved.

Exercise

The exercise for this chapter requires you to think about designing the first part of a study to investigate a particular language change which is said to be ongoing in Californian English, namely the lowering of lax front vowels (so *bit* sounds more like *bet*, and *bet* sounds more like *bat*). How would you design an experiment to test the hypothesis that front lax vowels are lowering in Californian English? Here are some things to think about:

a. What is meant by California English? (Is this change happening in Los Angeles and San Francisco, for example, or only in San Diego?)
b. How will you go about selecting participants in your study?
c. Will you record your participants?
d. How long will you spend collecting the data?
e. Will you make use of earlier research on this dialect area? Why (not)?

Further reading

Labov (1994, 2001) provides a detailed account of principles of linguistic change (both the internal mechanisms of sound change, and the external motivations associated with language use). McMahon (1994) provides a comprehensive account of language change, including specific discussion of the sociolinguistics of change, as does Aitchison (2001). Milroy (1992) is useful for an understanding of the relationship between network structure and change. Again, the *Handbook of Language Variation and Change* listed in the reading of the previous chapter provides a number of comprehensive summaries of research on the sociolinguistics of change. Eckert (1990) is an excellent article on the relationship between gender and linguistic change.

Note

1. Higher index scores represent more innovative pronunciations.

6 English historical sociolinguistics

6.1 Overview

We saw in Chapter 5 that an important contribution made by variationist sociolinguistics is to our understanding of how current linguistic variation in a community can be an indication of change in progress; and we saw in Chapter 4 that an important contribution made by traditional dialectology is to our understanding of how current linguistic variation can be an indication of the outcome of past changes. In this chapter we consider how present-day sociolinguistic methodology can be employed (with some important modifications) to historical data, to explain variation and change in the history of English. This discipline is sometimes known as historical sociolinguistics. Section 6.2 deals briefly with methodological issues – how do we interpret variation in the history of English, and how do we adapt the methods used by present-day sociolinguistics to understand variation and change in the past? Sections 6.3 to 6.6 deal with variation in each of the major periods of English: Old English (from the first Germanic invasions through to the Norman Conquest in the eleventh century CE); Middle English (up to the beginning of the sixteenth century CE); early Modern English (the sixteenth and seventeenth centuries CE) and late Modern English (from the eighteenth century CE to the present). One important issue must be borne in mind. While much of the discussion for the earlier history of English focuses unavoidably on the story of English in England, it is important to bear in mind that 'English' (however we define it) has always been a mongrel language, the result of a series of encounters with other linguistic varieties, which we will explore in more detail in Chapter 7. The myth of pure English is exactly that – a myth – and we discover this primarily by examining the social context in which speakers of varieties of English operated in the past.

6.2 Methodology

As we saw in Chapters 4 and 5, researchers interested in contemporary linguistic variation have paid a great deal of attention to the methods they use in collecting their data – which informants are selected, the discourse context in which the informants are recorded, how the recorded material is transcribed, are all issues that sociolinguists and dialectologists need to bear in mind. Similar – but not identical – concerns exist for historical linguists, who also need to concern themselves with an honest assessment of the appropriate methods of data collection.

One significant issue concerning the nature of the data collected in historical sociolinguistic studies is that the data are typically written, not spoken (unless we are looking at variation from the beginning of the twentieth century onwards), and that in many cases we know much less than we would like to about the author, the addressee, and the social context of the production of the text. This means that we only have access to the (small) proportion of people who in earlier times were able to write; and only a small proportion of the written record survives. This stands in sharp contrast to many of today's sociolinguistic studies, as we saw in Chapter 4: now, it is possible to discover a great deal about the individuals whose speech makes up the corpus for analysis, especially if one adopts a 'participant observation' approach to the initial data collection. When sociolinguists use such 'bad data' (see further Nevalainen and Raumolin-Brunberg 2003), it is therefore necessary to make adjustments in the methods used, and to recognise that we cannot adopt wholesale current sociolinguistic methodology when investigating historical material.

A further problem comes with the analysis of the linguistic data itself. It is clear that such evidence is useful for our understanding of aspects of linguistic variation in the earliest Englishes, but it is equally clear that interpreting and evaluating that evidence require a great deal of reconstruction on the part of the analyst: the variant spellings of a particular word may or may not be indications of different pronunciations of that word, and if they are, we cannot be certain as to what sound that spelling represents. It is possible to make a fair assessment of this sound–spelling correspondence, using established methods of historical linguistics, but it is obviously the case that such material is very different in kind from the tape recorded or digitally recorded data used in present-day sociolinguistic surveys. Furthermore, the fact that we are dealing with written language (not transcriptions of spoken language) must also be addressed, since conventions of written language (particularly with regard to clause structure) may be quite different to those of the spoken language.

None the less, there have been some studies which have attempted to apply modern sociolinguistic methods to historical data. A critical issue in historical sociolinguistics (and in historical linguistics in general) is the uniformitarian principle (see, for example, Labov 1994: 21–5 for discussion of this principle in linguistics and in other fields). This principle concerns motivations for change: it suggests that the linguistic forces which promote and check language change now are no different in kind from those which promoted and checked language change in the past. So if we witness a particular kind of change in contemporary English (for example, the vowel rotation known as Northern Cities Shift in North America, referred to in Chapter 5), then we can suggest that similar vocalic changes in the history of English follow similar principles – there is no reason to assume that mechanisms of change in the history of English were significantly different from mechanisms of change in contemporary English. In Chapter 5, the actuation, embedding and transmission of ongoing change were discussed. Most work in sociohistorical linguistics is concerned with the embedding of a change, and even more with the transmission of the change (that is, through different social networks, and in different stylistic contexts); again such approaches are typically found in studies where quantitative analyses are viable, which typically excludes the Old and Middle English periods. None the less, since there has been some work on Old English sociolinguistics, broadly defined, the next section explores variation in the earliest recorded forms of English.

6.3 Variation in Old English

While we have a range of different kinds of evidence for reconstructing Old English (OE) – runic carvings on stone crosses, such as that at Ruthwell in Dumfriesshire, glosses of charters granting tracts of land, such as those produced in the Canterbury scriptorium, and manuscripts of poems such as *Beowulf* – we still have comparatively little material to deal with. Furthermore, such texts have a widespread geographic provenance, and were composed at different points in the period of the language we know as Old English. This means that if we compare two OE 'texts' such as the Ruthwell Cross and a late entry in the *Anglo-Saxon Chronicle*, we are comparing two very different kinds of English: an analogy would be comparing a Shakespeare sonnet with a piece of twenty-first-century graffiti. OE dialectologists often refer to varieties of OE such as 'Northumbrian', 'Kentish' and 'West Saxon', but even taking into consideration the problems we have already identified in establishing what constitutes a dialect of a language in Chapter 1, OE dialects do not really correspond with geographical areas of the British Isles. They are more legitimately considered as text languages, varieties established by a set of shared features across a set of texts (and which are not shared by other sets of texts). Other evidence has none the less been adduced to establish dialect areas of OE, including placename evidence and variation in the spelling of names on coins.

As noted above, another of the major problems for any sociolinguistic account of the variation which emerges as a result of that reconstruction is our lack of knowledge about the speakers and writers involved, and the social context in which the speakers and writers operated. One thing we do know is that the majority of the texts that survive are the product of a specific social or cultural group, namely the aristocracy, or a religious order: see Hogg (2002: 115). In other words, we cannot reconstruct the language of women from the Old English period, or explore how ethnic divisions correlate with linguistic differences, in the way we can with present-day English varieties: we simply don't have the evidence to establish the correlations.

One thing we do know about many of the texts that have survived is that they were often composed in towns that functioned as centres for the Christian church in England (towns like Durham and Canterbury), and that of these centres, one reigns supreme as a source for the majority of extant texts: Winchester, in southern England. Texts produced in this area have come to be known as West Saxon texts, which are commonly divided into two diachronic periods, one around the time of King Alfred the Great (early West Saxon) in the latter part of the ninth century CE, and another around the time of the cleric and grammarian Ælfric, around the end of the tenth century CE (late West Saxon). What is particularly interesting about the writing of Ælfric is the fact that it displays little internal variation, and writing of a very similar kind can be found beyond the West Saxon area in the later Old English period. This lack of variation has led to the claim that the writing of Ælfric represented a kind of focused language (Hogg 2002: 126), alongside another focused variety, evident in texts from an area around the English West Midlands, which Hogg describes as 'Lichfield Mercian'. These varieties were certainly not as widespread or as codified as the Standard English of today, as we saw in Chapter 1; nor do we have evidence that they were reinforced by educational practice (for the few people who were formally educated at all) or other kinds of planning. Furthermore, the origins of the present-day (British) standard language are to be found not in the Winchester or Lichfield areas, but in the East Midlands and East Anglia; as Hogg (2002: 8) notes, there is very little evidence indeed from the Old English period to help us to trace the origins of our present-day standard variety. Yet the patterns which emerge in the history of the Old English dialects are of considerable interest to research on present-day dialect levelling, because we can see similar patterns in both periods (though the level of detail is much greater for contemporary English than it is for the earliest varieties).

Some current work on varieties of Old English has sought to bridge the gap between traditional dialectological methodology and more recent approaches to linguistic variation in a social context. Despite the problems we have established so far in this section, there have none the less been some attempts to correlate the spelling variation in some OE texts with what we know about the social milieu in which speakers and writers of OE operated: Toon (1983, 1992), for instance, has suggested that certain spelling changes which occurred in Kentish OE (associated with texts produced in the south-eastern part of England) in the ninth century are indicative of a sound change which began first in the Mercian region (a large area of the midlands of England), then spread to Kent as a result of the political influence which the Mercians exerted over the Kentish at the time. This research represents an interesting attempt to apply Labovian sociolinguistics to some of the earliest records of English, and would equate broadly with a 'change from above' as discussed in Chapter 5: a socially dominant group acts as a linguistic 'model' for a group of lower social status, who through a process of long-term accommodation may begin to adopt the linguistic features of the higher-status group. There are, however, problems with this account: there is not enough evidence to do detailed variationist work on the data; some of the historical accounts of the sociopolitical context in Kent at the time suggest that there may have been little opportunity for long-term accommodation between the Mercians and the Kentish; and the sound change which occurred in Kentish may be the result of contact not with Mercians but with immigrants from continental Europe in the ninth century. In later Kentish we witness the spread of West Saxon forms; and we can correlate this with a series of sociopolitical developments, including the establishment of a more unified Anglo-Saxon kingdom in opposition to the Danelaw (that is, the area under the control of the Danes, north-east of the old Roman road known as Watling Street, from London to Chester) – as the Wessex kingdom became more influential, so we see in the later extant Kentish texts a mixture of local and supra-local features, some of which show a significant majority of supra-local forms, just as our theories of present-day dialect contact would predict (see Chapter 8).

We can see similar issues relating to language contact in the history of the Northumbrian dialect (as manifest in texts produced in and around the city of Durham). For instance, the tenth-century CE gloss to the Lindisfarne Gospels (a magnificent illuminated manuscript produced on Lindisfarne, an island off the coast of Northumbria, in the late seventh or early eighth century CE) shows the adoption of some Old Norse forms which contrast with the forms we find in West Saxon texts. Moreover, these forms are grammatical items, not just lexical items (for example, the form *aron* 'are' as opposed to West Saxon *synd*; see Hogg 2002: 125): as we shall see in Chapter 7, when contact between different varieties is very substantial, the borrowings from one variety into another can involve forms from the grammatical system, in addition to lexical items. The effects on English of contact with speakers of Old Norse will be discussed in more detail in the following section.

So we see correlations between some aspects of the variation that we reconstruct for Old English, and some aspects of the social and political context that we reconstruct for Anglo-Saxon history. Such correlations are by no means as detailed as the correlations we are able to make for present-day varieties, but none the less reveal interesting possibilities for work on Old English dialects informed by sociolinguistic theory.

6.4 Variation in Middle English

It is sometimes tempting to think about attitudes towards varieties of English as being a more recent phenomenon, one which arose as a result of specific kinds of language planning in the modern period. However, such attitudes are discernible in the earlier history of the language, as the following example illustrates:

(1) Al þe longage of þe Norþhumbres, and specialych at ȝork, ys so scharp, slyttyng and frotying, and unschape, þat we Souþeron men may þat longage unneþe vndurstonde. Y trowe þat þat ys bycause þat a buþ nyȝ to strange men and aliens þat spekeþ strangelych, and also bycause þat þe kynges of Engelond woneþ alwey fer fram þat contray: for a buþ more y-turnd to the souþ. (John of Trevisa's translation of Higden's *Polychronicon*, 1382, cited in Lass 1999: 7)

(*Translation:* All the language of the Northumbrians, and especially in York, is so sharp, biting, piercing and misshapen that we Southern men cannot easily understand that language. I believe that that is because they are near to strange men and aliens that speak strangely, and also because (that) the kings of England always live far from that country: because they are more turned to [that is, concerned with] the south).

Although comments like these are useful for understanding the linguistic ideology of a particular person, because such comments are fairly infrequent in the extant documents, very little can be said about how widespread such views were.

None the less, one thing that a comment such as this suggests is that dialect variation was salient in Middle English (ME). Partly this follows from the absence of the same kind of standard language that we are accustomed to in contemporary English. There is little sense of a focused variety of ME (compare the earlier discussion of OE), except in a very few cases where the scribal traditions of OE were maintained. Furthermore, there is little indication – particularly in the early ME period – of a supra-local consensus on norms of usage. Indeed, if we want to talk about norms, the only thing we can claim is that variation was the norm in ME, even in fairly formal writing. Certainly it was the case that variation was tolerated more readily than it is in today's English. One thing that stands out about ME is the great diversity in the written language.

With all these issues in mind, it is still possible to make some observations about variation in ME that we might link to the social and political contexts in which English was used. One very important issue with regard to social change and English concerns the use of English itself. The Norman invasion of England brought a new style of government, with a new set of linguistic practices (including the use of Latin in official documents, and French in law courts), which had two particular effects: some marginalisation of English in the early ME period as a vernacular language, and an increase in new words for particular concepts. The degree of bilingualism in the early Middle English period is quite substantial, at least among the upper classes and the emergent merchant class, and as a result a new variety of Anglo-French emerges to become the prestige language in some formal domains (including government and law). Over time, the influence of French dwindles, with increased calls for English to be used in particular contexts (especially legal contexts), along with a resurgence of literature in English. Alongside this, in the fifteenth century, the influence of the London standard begins to grow, with fewer and fewer texts written in regional varieties: this process itself is enabled by the development of printing, and the adoption of increasingly uniform spellings in printed text.

As we will see in Chapter 7, when we talk of contemporary language contact, where varieties of English are transported beyond the British Isles, it is important to bear in mind that it is in fact different varieties of different languages that come into contact, and the same holds true for the history of the language within Britain. For example, both

Norman French and Parisian (or Central) French had an influence on ME. Phonological differences between the two varieties meant that what were in French regional variants became two different lexemes in ME. For instance, many words in Norman French that began with /w/ began with /g/ in Central French: this explains the lexical additions of a *warrant* and a *guarrant* (> Modern English *guarantee*), or a *warden* and a *guardian*.

As noted in the previous section, speakers of English had also been in regular contact with speakers of Scandinavian origin, from very early on in the history of the language, and we see the results of this contact most clearly in the ME period. The evidence suggests that the contact between these speakers is likely to have been substantial, because of the kind of borrowing that takes place. (This will be discussed in more detail in Chapter 7.) The borrowing from Old Norse involves more than just borrowing new words; it involves changes in the grammatical structure of some varieties. For instance, pronoun forms like *they* and *them* are borrowed from Old Norse, and these forms end up as part of the standard variety. Borrowings which survive into northern English dialects are more substantial (*garth* 'yard', *kirk* 'church'), and placenames in the north also attest to the strong Norse influence (for example, placenames ending in -*thorpe* 'village' or -*thwaite* 'paddock').

A final issue concerns whether or not the kind of evidence available to us allows for a variationist study of ME dialects. Certainly this has been attempted (see, for example, Milroy 1983 on H-Dropping in Middle English and the later history of the language); and the range of evidence we have for ME is greater than we have for OE. But it is still clear that the lack of evidence we have about the provenance of some of the data, and about the social characteristics of specific users of the language, means that the kind of quantitative work that can be done will need to be of a different kind to modern sociolinguistic surveys: the problems that hold for OE in this regard continue into ME.

6.5 Variation in early Modern English

It is from the early modern period on that applications of modern variationist sociolinguistics to the history of English have been most systematically and successfully made. At the same time, it is in the early modern period that we witness two important historical developments, one which led to focusing, and the other which led to diffusion. The first concerns the development of the standard language, reinforced by the increase in printed texts following the establishment of the printing press in England by William Caxton in 1476, noted above; the second concerns the spread of English beyond the British Isles, as settlers moved to North America, and trade routes developed across the globe. In this section we look at the following: the use of a corpus of private letters to explore patterns of linguistic variation in the period; the effects of printing and other social changes on the development of a standard language; and the establishment of 'new Englishes' across the globe.

In the early modern period, for the first time, we can begin to group together a significant number of texts from the same group of individuals according to genre. Genre is important since it relates to text structure, formality and the social context in which texts are created and used (Nevalainen and Raumolin-Brunberg 2003). The Corpus of Early English Correspondence (CEEC; for details, see Nevalainen and Raumolin-Brunberg 1996) is a computerised corpus of personal letters written by people whose individual histories are fairly well known to us. We are therefore able to group together individuals who are socially similar, and explore the extent to which they display similar linguistic practices. For instance, if we know that a given set of texts was written by a group of noblemen from the southern part of England, and another set was written by a group of socially mobile men from the same part of the country, and we observe that there are statistically significant differences in their linguistic practices, we can legitimately propose that such linguistic differences might be an indication of differing social status in the early modern period. Similar patterns may be attested for other speaker variables. On the basis of data from this corpus, researchers have discovered that, for example, women were the leaders in certain linguistic changes, including the development of *you* as the subject pronoun for second person plural (replacing the older form *ye*). Furthermore, the geographic diffusion of innovations is also attested in such a corpus: the spread of the -*s* ending on verbs (replacing -*th*), mentioned in Section 5.3, is an example of a northern English variant spreading to southern English in the late 1400s; it also seems to have been adopted more readily by lower-ranking groups, spreading to high-status groups only in the following century. Other northern features also seem to spread, regionally to London, and socially from lower classes to higher classes: these features include the use of *my* and *thy*, instead of *mine* and *thine* (Nevalainen 2006: 140–2). Such features are relevant to the standardisation of English, discussed in Chapter 3, and revisited briefly here.

It is in the early modern period that we first see English being established as an official language. This was a period of significant debate regarding the form and function of English. In addition to the debate about whether to use archaisms, or whether to use words borrowed from the classical languages (known as the Inkhorn debate: see

Nevalainen 1999, 2006), there were also calls for English to be recognised as an appropriate medium for academic discourse: Isaac Newton, for instance, wrote some of his scientific work in English (for example, *Opticks*, published in 1704) and some in Latin (for example, *Philosophiae Naturalis Principia Mathematica*, published in 1687). In this period there was also the establishment of clear links between language and nationhood. As England was developing as an international power, so English developed as an international language.

Attitudes towards different varieties of English – and the association of linguistic varieties with types of speaker – continued to be expressed in this period; and as disputes about the form and function of English grew, there were further observations which were alleged to characterise the language of particular groups. For example, we begin to see explicit criticism of the language of women in the early modern period, as exemplified by the following from Thomas Elyot, who is discussing what kind of language is appropriate in child rearing, suggesting nurses should:

(2) speke none englisshe but that whiche is cleane polite perfectly and articulately pronounced omittinge no lettre or sillable as folisshe women often times do of a wantonnesse wherby diuers noble men and gentilmennes chyldren (as I do at this daye knowe) haue attained corrupte and foule pronuntiation. (Thomas Elyot, 1531, *The Boke Named the Gouernour*, fol. 19v.)

In addition, it is in this period that we begin to see the extent of the spread of English beyond the British Isles. And just as the language of the Germanic tribes encroached further on the indigenous Celtic languages of Britain in the fifth century, pushing them further to the north and west of the British Isles, so the spread of English in North America began in a highly localised community on the north-east coast in the seventeenth century, and gradually spread westward, following trade routes and settlement patterns, encroaching on native American and (in some areas) Hispanic varieties. Contact with native American languages brought new lexical items into the language (for example, *racoon* and *squash*); and the contest between English and Spanish on the north and central American continent continues to this day. Further evidence of the incipient spread of global English comes from the range of source languages for words borrowed into English in this period. Examples (even if we restrict this to the set of animal names) include *flamingo* from Portuguese, *mammoth* from Russian, *jackal* from Turkish, *orang-utan* from Malay, and *mongoose* from Kannada.

6.6 Variation in late Modern English

Late Modern English (the English of the eighteenth to the twentieth centuries) was until recently a relatively under-researched period in the history of the language; yet it is this period in which we can observe the establishment of some of the practices which are still relevant to folk linguistics today. The late modern period is the one in which beliefs in 'correct' and 'proper' English came to the fore, and the one in which the notion of a standard language, mooted from the late Middle English period onwards, began to be most systematically developed.

The evidence we have in this period is substantial. Not only do we have examples of variation in writing (for example, between educated and uneducated writers) which we can use to reconstruct aspects of the pronunciation and grammar of the period, but we also have an increasingly large body of evidence *about* language, particularly about good and bad language (on which see also Chapter 1). This evidence needs to be treated with care (for example, some of the forms alleged to represent 'good' language may be very archaic, and spoken only by a very few highly educated people from a particular social class), but there is no doubt that this kind of evidence is much more substantial. Furthermore, we have the continuing representations of dialect in literature, as well as literature which is written entirely in a particular dialect. Again, such material should be analysed with caution, but can give a good idea of what features typified a particular region. However, just as was the case for the early Modern period, there is a need to distinguish between evidence we gather from the printed language, and that which comes to us from letters and other personal correspondence. The former is likely to reveal far less variation than the latter, because the former is focused, and highly standardised, while the latter is more diffuse.

The growth of linguistic ideology in the late modern period (Tieken-Boon van Ostade 2006; Mugglestone 2006) is one of the major effects of the codification of English in the eighteenth century. Specifically, there was a sense that the written language had become contaminated with variants from the spoken language, and, picking up on some of the views about the status of English expressed in the previous two centuries, some sought to demonstrate that English needed to be codified if it were to function as a national, prestigious language, comparable to Latin. This resulted in a significant growth in the publication of grammars, including that of Lindley Murray (who based much of his work on an earlier grammar by Robert Lowth). The popularity of Murray's grammar was substantial – not only was the grammar frequently reprinted within the

United Kingdom, but it was also translated into a number of languages, including French, Swedish and Japanese, thus marking "the beginnings of the spread of English as a world language" (Nevalainen and Tieken-Boon van Ostade 2006: 285).

One of the consequences of establishing a standard variety is that non-standard varieties typically becoming increasingly stigmatised. It was during the late modern period that criticisms of local varieties began to become increasingly frequent, because in many cases, the function of the grammar book was as a guide to correct usage – in order to point out what was the correct form, authors sometimes would specify a set of errors, often associated with particular regional varieties. Furthermore, we see increasing correlations between stigmatised language and types of speaker. For instance, in many cases, use of non-standard forms was said to be characteristic of women (Tieken Boon van Ostade 2006: 259), often on the grounds that they had not received the same kind of education as men. Taking both regional and social provenance together, and borrowing terms from both Wales (2006) and Coates (1993) respectively, we can suggest that the codification of the standard language in England was increasingly both austrocentric (focused on the language of the south) and androcentric (focused on the language of men).

So far we have been addressing subnational varieties of English, within what is now the United Kingdom, and predominantly English English. But we have also seen that in this period English was spreading beyond the British Isles, and in these newly established English-speaking communities, we see quite a different story. In many cases British English was seen to be deficient, not fit for purpose for a new world. A good example of a proponent of this ideology is Noah Webster, who campaigned for reform of English in the newly independent United States:

(3) As an independent nation, our honor requires us to have a system of our own, in language as well as government. Great Britain . . . should no longer be our Standard. (Webster, *Dissertation on the English Language*, 1789)

Note again how this is an issue of ideology: a new variety for a new nation. This was marked most prominently by a codified spelling reform. Some of Webster's reforms did become conventionalised in American English – for example, using <er> instead of <re> in words like *center*, <or> instead of <our> in words like *color*, and -*ize* instead of -*ise* as a verb forming suffix (e.g. *generalize*) – but not all did (e.g. *tun* for *ton*).

6.7 The future of English?

Having explored the aspects of English historical sociolinguistics from the Germanic invasions to the present day, I now turn to the question of how varieties of English might develop in the future, based on some of the incipient developments of today. This is important, because in many textbooks on the history of English, there is a sense that the 'English' of today is really not that different from the English of 1800 (and presumably therefore unlikely to change radically in the future);[1] however, this is a fallacy. The standard written variety of British or American English, for example, may not have varied greatly since its extensive codification; but the spoken language has continued to evolve, and the development of electronic communications has revolutionised the way in which English is used around the globe. Again, the social context of English in use helps us to understand the variable shape of the language as it changes to suit the needs of its users.

One significant aspect of the English of the future is its current global status. As Crystal (2003: 189) observes, "[t]here has never been a language so widely spread or spoken by so many people as English". Because of its widespread use around the world at the beginning of the twenty-first century, comparisons have been made between English and the medieval 'global' language, Latin. There are a number of interesting parallels. Particularly, one of the things that has been suggested is that English will fracture into distinct, mutually unintelligible varieties ('languages'), just as vulgar Latin developed into Romance languages such as Italian, Romanian and Catalan. One of the forces that might drive such a development is the increasing number of speakers of English as a second or other language: in fact, the number of such speakers outnumbers speakers of English as a first language by a ratio of three to one (McArthur 2006; Crystal 2006a).

But a further parallel is equally important. In the early modern period, speakers of English made use of Latin in particular registers, but they often did not simply borrow the Latin form wholesale. They anglicised Latin, by changing some of the inflectional endings – for instance, the -us ending on terrificus was dropped to form the 'English' word terrific; similarly, as English is the global language of the current period, speakers of other languages modify and shape English words to make them fit the shape of their own language. For example, the borrowing of some words from English into African languages means that stress patterns need to be reassigned. English is a stress-timed language (the time interval between stressed syllables is roughly the same), whereas Zulu is a syllable-timed language (the time interval between syllables is roughly the same, irrespective of stress); as Crystal (2006a: 396) observes, when a proper noun like *South Africa* is borrowed by speakers of Zulu, each syllable receives the same degree of stress, unlike in English. Furthermore, just as the use of Latinate vocabulary came to have a special social function for speakers of English (the association with educated status, for example), so using English fulfils a local social function in the contemporary societies in which it is used.

A further important development concerns the use of English as the medium for many kinds of electronic communication, as noted in Chapter 2. One reason that e-English is fascinating for sociolinguists is that it is said to record the 'voices' of groups which are traditionally under-represented in the study of variation and change in the history of the language (Crystal 2006a). However, just as is the case for all the kinds of evidence we have looked at in this chapter and elsewhere in this book, from Anglo-Saxon monuments, through personal letters in the sixteenth century, to digital recordings of people speaking, we must treat such evidence with caution, and interrogate it. For example, the identities of participants in a chatroom may not be what they appear to be, and someone who claims to be a 14-year-old boy from London might well be a 50-year-old woman from San Francisco. In other words, we cannot be sure that the text we are reading definitely comes from an author who claims to have a particular set of social attributes. Equally, the dominance of English as the language of the web may be beginning to fade: the proportion of internet hosts in English dropped to less than 70 per cent by 2003 (Crystal 2006b: 431) – as Crystal observes, however, this does not necessarily mean that exposure to English via the web is decreasing, because particular sites in English may still be getting the largest number of hits.

6.8 Summary

In this chapter we have looked at how we might consider applying sociolinguistic methods and principles to historical data from varieties of English. We saw that this process of application becomes harder the further back in history we go. English historical sociolinguistics is a growing field of research, from work on language attitudes to quantitative studies. Different kinds of problems appear when we try to analyse data from different 'periods' of English, so again we see the importance of a rigorous method for this kind of research.

Exercise

Here is an example of a text from the early Modern English period (Wilson, *The Arte of Rhetorique*, 1553), which describes a particular attitude towards the way in which English was perceived to be changing:

> Some seke so farre for outlandishe Englishe, that thei forget altogether their mothers langage. And I dare swere this, if some of their mothers were aliue, they were not able to tell, what thei say, & yet these fine Englishe clerkes, wil saie thei speake in their mother tongue, if a man should charge them for counterfeityng the kynges English. Some farre iornied ientlemen at their returne home, like as thei loue to go in forrein apparell, so thei wil pouder their talke w^t ouersea language. He that cometh lately out of France, wil talke Frenche English, & neuer blushe at the matter. Another choppes in with Angleso Italiano.

> (*Translation:* Some seek so far for outlandish English, that they altogether forget their mother tongue. And I'd swear to this: if some of their mothers were alive, they would not be able to understand what they say, and yet these fine English students will say they speak in their mother tongue, if a person should charge them with counterfeiting the King's English. Some well-travelled gentlemen, when they return home, just as they like to dress in foreign clothes, so they will sprinkle their talk with foreign language. He that comes recently from France will talk French English and never blush at so doing. Another chops in with Angleso Italiano.)

To what extent is this kind of language attitude still present today, regarding the influence of other languages on English? To what extent are complaints more to do with the failure to conform to standard English norms? What evidence can you find of earlier or later examples of attitudes towards changes in the form of English?

Further reading

The main text for work on quantitative historical sociolinguistics is Nevalainen and Raumolin-Brunberg (2003), which deals with methodological and analytical issues, using data from the CEEC. The *Cambridge History of the English Language* (six volumes, 1992–2001, general editor Richard Hogg) contains a wealth of information about variation in English at different periods. Tieken-Boon van Ostade (2000) discusses some of the normative approaches to language which characterise aspects of the recent history of English. Mugglestone (2003) is another valuable book on the sociolinguistics of the recent history of English. The history-of-English books which are already published in this series (Hogg 2002, Horobin and Smith 2002 and Nevalainen 2006) all deal with variation in the period they are investigating.

Note

1. See Mugglestone (2006: 278–88) for a discussion of what she terms 'myths of stasis' in the English of recent times.

7 Language contact

i match program sono on-line!
Taken from the website of the Italian football club Inter Milan (www.
inter.it), accessed 9 December 2007

7.1 Overview

This chapter is concerned with contact between speakers of mutually
unintelligible varieties. It begins with a discussion of some pidgin and
creole varieties which have emerged as a result of contact involving
speakers of English and speakers of other languages. There is also a
discussion of code-switching, a common feature of bilingual speakers,
who regularly move between two languages in everyday discourse with
other bilingual speakers. There is finally some discussion of the advantages and disadvantages of English as a global language.

7.2 Pidgin and creole varieties

One of the possible outcomes of a linguistic situation in which speakers
of English come into regular contact with speakers of other languages is
that a new variety – or series of varieties – may emerge. This is a kind
of language change, but a rather special one, because this new variety
emerges rather rapidly. Although Old English looks very different from
contemporary Standard English, we can see the gradual transmission
from one stage to the next, given the wealth of documentary evidence
we have for British English. Labels such as 'Old English' and 'Middle
English' are labels of convenience for linguists, in an attempt to package
the history of the language into chunks that correlate with particular
linguistic or cultural developments. The change from one stage to
another is almost imperceptible. But this is not the case with varieties
that emerge as a result of contact between speakers of very different
languages.

The label linguists give to a variety often correlates with the function of that variety in the community in which it emerges, and the extent to which users of the variety tend to converge on a series of norms. Sometimes, contact produces a variety which shows great heterogeneity from speaker to speaker, which has very little in the way of a systematic grammar, and a great deal of variation in the lexical items used to refer to the same concept: this is often known as a jargon.

In a large number of cases, the contact variety is more systematic, with a greater stability in the linguistic system and in the series of lexical choices. This too may involve a jargon, at least initially; but if the jargon is the only 'common ground' for speakers who do not otherwise understand one another, that jargon takes on an increased burden for communicative purposes. The jargon then typically stabilises, and the speakers typically agree on a series of linguistic conventions. The pidgin variety which emerges does so in a context where the users of the pidgin have another set of linguistic resources (via their first language) to fulfil the roles that the pidgin does not: in other words, the pidgin functions as an auxiliary language, often with a very specific function (for example, to facilitate trade).

In cases where a stable pidgin is frequently used in a community, the children born into that environment may find that their primary input, as they are acquiring language, is the pidgin; and because the pidgin is comparatively limited (in function and in form), the children develop the pidgin, which becomes more complex grammatically, and which carries a larger functional load (for example, instead of simply using it to facilitate trade, speakers use features of the more complex pidgin to mark social identity). When a pidgin variety develops in this way – becoming formally more complex, increasing its sociolinguistic burden – and especially when it becomes the 'first language' of a new generation, the emergent variety is known as a creole.

This standard trajectory of jargon > pidgin > creole was quite a common story in creolistics (the study of pidgin and creole languages), but did rather oversimplify things. One particular problem, for instance, is the heterogeneity of many creole varieties, and the very different formal properties they have, even when they have emerged in similar social contexts (Mufwene 2006).

Pidgins and creole languages are interesting to a number of different kinds of linguists (McWhorter 2003): some linguists are interested in pidgins and creoles because they provide interesting evidence relating to language acquisition, for instance, while others use data from pidgins and creoles to test hypotheses about constraints on language change. Many sociolinguists are interested in pidgins and creoles because they provide evidence regarding the social correlations of language use, and because many pidgin languages emerge in similar kinds of social context: for example, many pidgin languages are found in coastal regions, and emerged in trade colonies in a period of significant political and economic expansion of a number of European powers in the seventeenth to nineteenth centuries.

We can ask what role English has played, and continues to play, in the formation of pidgins and creoles. Because pidgin and creole varieties often emerge in similar social and economic contexts, there are many formal similarities which are said to exist across pidgins and creoles that are found in diverse geographical locales. Some pidgins and creoles are formed as a result of contact between a European language other than English (for example, French or Portuguese) and one or more local languages, but we will concentrate on cases where English is the non-local language used. The role played by the local language and English in forming the pidgin is usually slightly different: the local languages often provide more of the basic grammatical framework (the sound system and the syntactic patterns), with more of the vocabulary taken from English. But it is important to be aware that this is an issue of general weighting: it is certainly not the case that in Papua New Guinea, for example, where the well-known pidgin variety of Tok Pisin emerged, all of the grammatical features came from the local languages like Tolai, and all of the words came from English. Language contact is never as simple as that. What we see is a larger proportion of the words coming from English (which is said to be the lexifier for Tok Pisin) than from the local languages; conversely, more of the grammatical features come from the local languages. However, as is often the case in language change, lexical items taken from the lexifier may come to serve an increasingly grammatical function. For instance, in Bislama, spoken in Vanuatu, the pronoun system includes two distinct forms for first person plurals, equivalent to two possible meanings of *we* in contemporary British English. The first is *mifala i*, which means 'me and more than two other people, but not you' and the other is *yumi*, which means 'you (three or more) and me' (Meyerhoff 2006: 257). The first of these is a combination of the pronoun *me*, the noun *fellow* and the pronoun *he*, which has acquired a particular grammatical function in this variety. (Incidentally, if you are a monolingual speaker of English, it might strike you as strange to think of a language having two different first person plural pronouns, but in fact, this was the case in Old English.)

Given the complex interplay between the different languages involved in the creation of pidgin and creole varieties, then, it would be inaccurate to think of them as varieties of English (and even worse to think of them as bad or faulty varieties of English). This is not only because of the various social and political issues we addressed in Chapter 3; they are also formally very different. Furthermore, we can identify degrees of difference *within* a creole, depending on the extent to which there is divergence from Standard English. The variety which approximates most closely to the standard is known as the acrolect; that which diverges most is known as the basilect; and the myriad varieties which are located somewhere along that continuum are known as mesolects.

7.3 Some features and examples of English-lexifier pidgins and creoles

Many contact languages show simplification in their early stages, and this may change or may continue. This typically involves a reduction in a number of linguistic features that may be redundant, or superfluous to the basic needs of communication. Consider a standard English expression like *three weeks*: in this example, the *-s* ending of *weeks* is superfluous (since plurality is already marked by *three*) – so one way of simplifying this would be to say *three week*. This and other kinds of simplification can be commonly found in pidgin languages: for instance, case marking may disappear (so there is no distinction between a subject pronoun like *I* and an object pronoun like *me*, and speakers rely on word order to make the necessary distinctions, as in *mi kam*), along with other kinds of inflectional morphology (so that possession, sometimes coded in standard English with an inflectional clitic *'s*, as in *John's house*, may be coded in a pidgin language via the syntax, using particular words (as in *haus bilong John*). Other instances of reduction include a limited set of lexical items. However, these can be combined in innovative ways, often making use of our cognitive predilection for metaphor. For instance, concepts like 'grass', 'moustache' and 'eyebrow' all involve a collection of individual 'shoots' that are perceived as a whole – the first (and most basic) grows in the ground, the second grows above the mouth, and the third along the top of the eye. This perhaps explains the forms *gras*, *mausgras* (= mouthgrass) and *gras antap long ai* (= grass on-top along eye), meaning 'grass', 'moustache' and 'eyebrow', respectively, in Tok Pisin (Romaine 1988: 35). Phonological reduction is also common in pidgin languages – most typically, this involves a reduction in the number of phonological contrasts (phonemes) in the variety.

Does this reduction make pidgins easier to understand? The answer to this question is 'no', which is perhaps surprising, given the fact that we said that pidgins often arose in situations where speakers needed to communicate with each other yet did not share a common language.

Simplification is essentially a benefit for the speaker, rather than the hearer, who has to rely on more contextual cues (understanding the pragmatics of the communicative act) in order to interpret the message. For instance, if a pidgin language dispenses with copular verbs (for example, *he out* for 'he is/was out'), the speaker's production burden is decreased, but the hearer's processing burden is increased, since the hearer needs to rely either on context, or on pragmatics, to establish whether the speaker is referring to a present or past state.

Creole languages start to shift in the other direction, showing an increase in lexical items, more grammatical/inflectional morphology, increased syntactic complexity, and growth of phonological contrasts. This development – from a state of initial diffuseness (jargon), we then get an increase in focusing (pidgin), then a state involving more diffuseness (creole) – is an important one, which we will return to in the next chapter, which considers dialect contact.

So far I have concentrated primarily on the forms of these contact varieties, and stressed that it can be hard to distinguish between a pidgin and a creole on formal grounds. We can talk about either end of the continuum to highlight gross differences, but it is important not to forget the fact that this is a continuum. This continuum is perhaps made clearer when we consider the various functions of pidgin and creole languages. For example, it is the case that creoles often have a wider functional load than 'typical' pidgins; but it is often the case that pidgins which fulfil a variety of social functions (being much more than a trade language, and used in wider social contexts) come to serve as creoles in particular communities. A further ramification of this increase in the sociolinguistic contexts of use is an increase in sociolinguistic variability (where speakers who are members of the creole community increasingly tend to agree on norms, and evaluate variability in the same way); but this too may be incipient in a pidgin that has been stable for some time. Yet again we are faced with the problem of discreteness in defining linguistic concepts – distinguishing between a pidgin and a creole is as problematic as distinguishing a language from a dialect. We can use both formal and functional criteria to make gross categorisations at either end of the continuum, but the real situation is usually much more fuzzy.

Here is an example of a contact variety, using data collected from speakers on the island of St Vincent (the extract and translation are taken from Le Page and Tabouret-Keller 1985: 90):

(1) won de, nansi wen dong tukuma gu tel aal dem gyel hau he doz raid bru lai-an. Wel bru lai-ai didn fiil su veri pliiz abaut dat su neks taim

wen i sii brer nansi i aks brer nansi hau i kud gu aut tukuma gu tel aal dem gyel hau i doz raid om.

(*Translation*: One day, Anansi went down to Tukuma to go and tell all those girls how he was accustomed to ride Brother Lion. Well, Brother Lion didn't feel so very pleased about that so next time when he saw Brother Anansi he asked Brother Anansi how he could go out to Tukuma and tell all those girls how he was accustomed to ride him.)

From this example, it is clear that English is the lexifier, but there are a great many distinctive grammatical features (as well as some phonological features suggested by the spellings, such as *aal, dem, gyel* and *aks*). For instance, there is no infinitive marker *to* to indicate purpose (*wen dong tukuma gu tel*); there is a reduction in the number of distinct morphological forms of verbs, so that we understand *sii* and *aks* to mean 'saw' and 'asked' (that is, the past tense of *see* and *ask*, respectively) from the context; similarly, there is no plural marking on the form for 'girls' (*gyel*), because plurality can be inferred from the quantifier *aal* 'all'. Also, there is an interesting use of the auxiliary verb *do* (in this variety, *doz*) to mark habitual aspect, so *doz raid* 'does ride' means something like 'is accustomed to, or regularly rides'.

7.4 Code-switching

A further feature of language contact is the notion of code-switching, a term used to describe the linguistic situation where a speaker will alternate between two varieties (or codes) in conversation with others who have a similar linguistic repertoire. Yet again in such cases we are required to consider not only the form that such switches take, but also the function of the variation. Sometimes we can witness switches that seem to involve just one word:

(2) ƛáq'ʷ   kʷit   'úxˠw   š-ʔul'   store...   ši -c
    good   2SG.PERF go   LOC-to   store   INDIR -1SG.OBJ
    'Will you go to the store for me please?' (Rowicka 2005: 314)

This utterance comes from a speaker of Quinault, a Native American language spoken on the north-west coast of the United States; the speaker was also a near-native English speaker, though she acquired English as a second language. This innocent-looking example is actually quite revealing. Many sociolinguists who study code-switching recognise differences between genuine instances of switching and other instances where only one word is borrowed. For example, if I said:

(3) I ate a croissant for breakfast.

it would be a questionable claim to suggest that I was code-switching between French and English, because it looks as though I have simply used what was a French word in a conventional English sentence. But the Quinault example in (2) is interesting not so much because of the word *store*, but rather because of the form which follows it. In Quinault and related languages, the *-ši* form usually only attaches to verbs; its appearance after the locative phrase (glossed as 'to store' in (2)), rather than directly after the Quinault form for *go*, leads Rowicka (2005: 314) to suggest that this speaker's command of English has led to changes in her Quinault grammar. In other words, long-term use of English as a second or other language may lead to subtle grammatical shifts in a speaker's first language.

A more extended example of code-switching, this time in an Italian American community, is provided in (4). In this extract, the symbol ::: marks an elongated sound, and // marks overlapping speech.

(4) 01 Enzo: ((beats his hand on the table and laughs looking at Carlo)) I'm not

02 gonna say anything, Carlo!

03 Carlo: *No:::!*

04 ((to Peter)) *Cosa fai? Ma cosa fai? Adesso che hai messo giù la carta hai*

05 *fatto così o hai bussato?* [What are you doing? But what are you doing?

Now that you have put that card down did you do that by chance or did you knock?]

06 Peter: *Ho // bussato!* [I knocked]

07 Enzo: *// Ha bussato!* [He knocked]

08 Carlo: Ok, good! *Quello che vogliamo sapere noi.* [That's what we want to know]

09 Enzo: ((Looking at Peter)) *I tempi di questo gioco* [the timing of this game]

10 ((looking at Carlo)) I've got to tell him because otherwise he's never

11 gonna learn it!

12 Carlo: I know!

13 Enzo: ((to Peter)) *Il primo gioco ho fatto io, il primo gioco dove l'ho fatto io?*

14 *Dove ho bussato io?* [I did the first move, the first move where did I do it?

Where did I knock?]
15 Peter: *Non ricordo.* [I can't remember]

(de Fina 2007: 381–2)

In her analysis of this discourse, in which Peter (born in America, but quite fluent in Italian) is being taught how to play a particular card game by Carlo and Enzo (both born in Italy, moved to America as adults, and fluent in English), de Fina (2007) observes that the linguistic patterns are a subtle reflection of changing patterns of interaction, where, for example, Italian is typically used where the speakers are explaining aspects of the card game, and English used for clarification and justification of actions. Note that Peter (who has Italian as a second language) none the less speaks in Italian to both Carlo (line 06) and Enzo (line 15); similarly, Carlo uses English in addressing Enzo (line 10) and Enzo uses English in addressing Carlo (lines 01–02), despite the fact that both of them have Italian as a first language. The negotiation of the discourse comes to be indexed by the very act of switching, as much as by the particular words and phrases used.

Sometimes speakers of English will choose to use other languages in a particular communicative act, even if they are not fluent speakers of that other variety (and may only know a handful of words or phrases). This is frequently seen in multilingual communities where English is the official language (either *de facto* or *de jure*), and a very good example of this is the kind of switching among adolescents which has been described as crossing (Rampton 1999). Rampton has defined crossing as "the use of a language or a variety that, in one way or another, feels anomalously 'other'" (Rampton 1999: 55). Crossing is seen as a particularly performative aspect of code-switching, because it is often attested in discourse in which verbal play is paramount, like joke telling, or light-hearted verbal abuse. In fact, the term 'code-pilfering' might be better than 'code-switching', because it characterises the fact that the code that is used in crossing somehow doesn't belong to the speaker who uses it, and that they only take a little bit of that code on any given occasion. Again, then, the issue of identity comes into play – but here, the very self-conscious nature of the switching means that the speaker is deliberately drawing attention to the projection of a particular identity, and most crucially, one that is not associated with the speaker's identity. To that extent, then, crossing is much less subtle than the other indexes of identity that we have discussed elsewhere in this book (for example, variation in the use of (p), (t) and (k) in Middlesbrough English in Chapter 4).

Our final example of code-switching comes not from speech, but from writing. The following example (taken from Bhatt 2008:190) is an advertisement for bread:

(5)

Bakwaas Advertising
First Class Bread
Gharam Dharam called me. Asked "Did you see Bhagat Singh"
I said mubaraka Deol saab. Bacchas have done a good thing
Sunny learnt acting from me. He was a beeba baccha
I have seen him pee in pants. Do poopoo in his kaccha
Bobby was not even born then. Bobby is our nyana
I have so many times scolded him for not eating his khana
He used to love suji da halwa and matter wali rice
Mostly I would feed him Harvest Gold de slice

Harvest Gold
Delhi's no. 1 Bread
(Bhatt 2008: 190)

As Bhatt observes, a full understanding of this text depends very much on a deep awareness of language and culture in multilingual India, and much of the humour in the advertising derives from the ability to 'read' the text on a number of levels. For example, the word *bakwaas* is a Hindi/Punjabi word meaning 'bad' or 'third-rate'; this is aligned in a parallel structure with the English 'first class', which leads Bhatt to suggest the advertisers may be playing on stereotypes regarding the attitudes towards English (first class) and Hindi/Punjabi (third rate) held by some Indians. There are further hints at the close interaction of different languages in India in this example (for instance, the use of an English suffix -*s* to mark plurality, attaching to a Hindi word (*baccha*+*s* = 'boys'). Taken as a whole, Bhatt suggests that the code-switching in this text "involves the embedding of local meanings in the global medium" (Bhatt 2008: 191). The tension between the global and the local in cases of contact with English is the subject of the final section of this chapter.

7.5 Deanglicisation and conventionalisation

Some evidence from English historical sociolinguistics discussed in Chapter 6 suggested that it has frequently been the case that some varieties of English are judged as being 'better' than others, to the extent that some believe in a 'correct' variety of English, with departures from that norm being labelled errors. This is seen not only in non-standard dialects of English spoken by 'native speakers', but also in the varieties that emerge when speakers of a language other than English acquire English at a later stage in their lives: that is, speakers of English as a second or other language. However, what are sometimes classed as errors (because they do not conform to a particular standard) often become conventionalised in local speech communities, and accepted as norms for the purposes of those communities. Crystal (2006a: 397) gives the example of the phrase *Welcome in Egypt*, where the choice of *in* over *to* is said to be influenced by the Arabic spoken in that community. Previously considered a mistake, it is now used by both native English speakers and native Arabic speakers as a norm, even codified as a local variant in EFL (English as a Foreign Language) textbooks for the Egyptian market. The fact that it is used by both groups suggests it could be seen legitimately as a product of linguistic accommodation. This may in part be associated with some of the advantages and drawbacks involved in the spread of English across the globe (see also Chapter 3).

On one side, those who argue that the global spread of English is a good thing focus on the fact that competence in English allows access to knowledge and to resources. In this view, English is enabling and empowering, giving people educational and commercial opportunities which would be restricted if only the language of the local community were used. On the other, it has been suggested that English is simply another way in which a particular community can be controlled and exploited. A parallel is often made with political and economic globalisation (Phillipson 1992): a relatively small group of powerful westerners come to dominate, not only through the political and economic system, but also through the cultural system (manifest most strongly, of course, through language). The spread of English in the British Isles resulted in the geographical marginalisation of indigenous Celtic languages to the north and west of the land mass. But this marginalisation is not simply geographical: it is also cultural and social, and the spread of English beyond the British Isles sometimes goes hand in hand with the imposition of a set of cultural norms by the colonising powers. If English comes to be the language of government, education, and business in a community, then local languages become restricted to specific domains (sometimes restricted just to the home); as the functional load of English increases in scope, the functional load of the local language narrows. This is not stable bilingualism – this is language shift, leading to the ultimate dominance of English across all domains in the community.

But sometimes this is not what happens. Speakers do one (or both) of two things, both of which are again connected to the notion of identity which we have appealed to throughout this book. One option is to maintain the local language, protecting its use in particular domains, and engaging in some kind of language planning that ensures the community recognises and values the cultural knowledge associated with the local variety. Many sociolinguists who work with speakers of languages that are endangered, or not yet codified, consider it part of the 'deal' struck when they record the speakers for their research, that they make some contribution to the protection of the local variety, by writing grammars or dictionaries of the language under investigation. A second option is to take 'English' and make it local. This practice (not always a conscious one) is what is currently giving rise to the increasingly distinctive 'new Englishes' (see Crystal 2003: 140–6) in various parts of Asia, for example, to the extent that speakers of these varieties may not easily understand one another (using the mutual intelligibility criterion, they would be speaking different languages). As noted in Chapter 6, a similar pattern is observable in the history of Latin: not only did the network bonds of speakers of vulgar Latin become so weak that new varieties emerged (for example, Italian, French, Spanish), but even in communities where Latin was the language of education and law, and not the language of interpersonal domains (for example, in medieval England), many words originating from Latin became 'vernacularised'. In other words, the norms in the communities in which 'new Englishes' are spoken may not derive from the practices and principles of the native speaker of English in the United Kingdom or the United States, but from those using the language in a particular local setting, for a particular set of communicative purposes, and for the negotiation of particular identities (Graddol 1999). Furthermore, a similar 'vernacularisation' takes place in situations of dialect contact, as we will see in the next chapter. If differences between languages and dialects are primarily social in nature, then we should expect similar processes and outcomes in the vernacularisation of different varieties of English around the world, whether we are talking about the evaluation of 'American' variants in New Zealand English, or 'English' variants in Hindi.

This is a very important feature of English sociolinguistics – the tension between the status of English as a *lingua franca*, and the emergence of new Englishes. As English develops rapidly in the world (on which see further Graddol 2006), it comes to serve a utilitarian function (where two individuals who don't speak each other's language may decide to communicate in English), so that it rather perversely could be described as an auxiliary language. Further consequences for the global spread of English are potentially highly significant. Two varieties of English (namely American and British English) have up until the beginning of the present century served as the models for learners of English as a foreign language. But this may no longer be the case in the future. Much rests on the extent to which new varieties of English gain wider recognition and status. In order to describe different kinds of English in different communities across the world, Kachru (1985) uses the idea of concentric circles:[1] at the heart of 'English' are the inner-circle varieties (such as those spoken in the UK, Australia and Canada), where, taking the population as a whole, English is the primary language; beyond this are the outer-circle varieties (such as are spoken in Singapore and India), where English was used by colonising powers in the past, and now has some official status, as we saw in Chapter 3; and finally, there are the expanding-circle varieties (such as those spoken in Germany and Japan), where there is no history of colonisation, but given the global spread of English, the language is often taught as the first 'foreign' language in schools, and may also be used in some media (see Schneider 2007 for an alternative account of the spread of English across the world).

Some of the outer-circle varieties of English have become so well established, and distinct from one another, that new names have been created to describe them, such as *Singlish* (Singaporean English) and *Hinglish* (Hindi + English). The possible issue here is what will happen if such varieties become the models for English as a foreign language: the more such varieties are legitimised, the more likely it is that these new Englishes will serve as models. But this is perhaps less likely given the function of English as a *lingua franca*. When English is used in such contexts, often adherence to the formal properties of a particular variety is of less concern to the interlocutors than is the need to communicate efficiently and display solidarity through consensus on a particular choice of language. In a sense, any old English will do, as long as the message gets across, and the appropriate social bond is created. Such a situation highlights yet again the myth of 'English' – we saw this in the discussion of the history of the language from Old English to the present, and we see it again in the diversification of English across the globe.

7.6 Summary

A remarkable feature about English has been its spread across the globe, but this can sometimes be rather exaggerated. First, it is not the case that 'one' English has been transported, but rather a selection of Englishes. These Englishes have diversified in contact with other languages, making them yet more distinct from the emergent standard. At the same time, the adoption of English as the world's *lingua franca* in particular contexts has meant that proficiency in a global standard – one that is functional irrespective of the location in which it is used, and irrespective of the other linguistic varieties used by the speakers of that standard – has become a valuable commodity for some, and has resulted in a further spread of the language in particular domains, in particular communities. That said, it is important not to forget that many humans in the world may never use any form of English; and those that do so may not see such variants as 'English', but rather as means to enrich their linguistic repertoire, and consequently the pool of resources to draw on in any given communicative act.

Exercises

The exercises for this chapter are discussion topics.

1. What are some of the motivations for code-switching?

2. To what extent is crossing similar to code-switching, and to what extent is it different?

3. Can a creole be distinguished from a pidgin purely on the basis of a set of formal properties?

Further reading

There are many books on contact linguistics and pidgin and creole languages, such as: Le Page and Tabouret-Keller (1985), Romaine (1988), Mühlhäusler (1997), Sebba (1997), Singh (2000), Thomason (2001), Winford (2003), and Mufwene (2008). A useful collection of articles on code-switching is Auer (1998), and a detailed monograph is Myers-Scotton (1997).

Note

1. While this model of concentric circles is useful for establishing large-scale differences, there is some gradience and overlap between 'inner' and 'outer' varieties, and between 'outer' and 'expanding' varieties.

8 Dialect contact

8.1 Overview

In the previous chapter, we considered some of the ways in which contact between speakers of mutually intelligible varieties could result in the emergence of new varieties known as pidgins and creoles. We also considered some of the social psychological motivations for accommodation, and illustrated how accommodation is associated with the development of contact languages. Many of the new Englishes have emerged as a result of patterns of long-term contact between transported varieties of English, and various indigenous languages across the globe.

But what happens when speakers of different dialects come into contact? If, as we argued in Chapter 1, there is no formal, linguistic difference between a dialect and a language (that is, if the distinction is primarily a functional, social one), then we would expect to see similar kinds of linguistic patterns emerging in cases of dialect contact to those we see in cases of language contact. In other words, the study of dialects in contact should prove to be a useful test case for some of the earlier claims. The degree of difference between the input and output varieties might be reduced in comparison with language contact scenarios; but the key issue is whether the general patterns and principles are the same.

We will begin our examination of the principles of dialect contact by considering some patterns in the dialects of Britain, before moving to the establishment of new varieties of English in the United States and in New Zealand. It is also important to understand some of the differences between what appear to be very similar processes associated with dialect contact.

8.2 Dialect contact in Britain

One useful distinction to make is that of endogenous vs. exogenous change. Endogenous change is concerned with the 'internal' development of a particular variety (that is, changes which occur that seem to be highly localisable to a given accent or dialect); exogenous changes are ones which are brought about primarily through contact with other accents and dialects. Trudgill (1999b) provides an account of endogenous and exogenous changes which have affected the variety of English spoken in and around Norwich. An example of an endogenous change concerns the vowel in the TRAP lexical set (that is, in words such as *trap, bat* and *sack*). In Norwich English, the vowel has been shown to undergo a diphthongisation to [aɛ] – this development is not attested either in Received Pronunciation (a British accent associated with upper-class and upper-middle-class speech) or in neighbouring local accents in the east of England, so it seems to be special to Norwich; it is one of the ways in which this particular accent is diverging from other accents, and thereby making Norwich English more distinctive (that is, it is an instance of dialect divergence).

An example of exogenous change concerns development of H-Dropping (a feature which was discussed in Chapter 4) in East Anglia in the mid-to-late twentieth century. H-Dropping, as we saw, is a salient feature of some varieties of English, and has been stigmatised for some time. Despite this, there is evidence from Trudgill's sociolinguistic studies carried out in Norwich (for example, Trudgill 1974, 1999b) to suggest that H-Dropping is on the increase in that area of England. East Anglia was one of the few areas of England not to have noticeable H-Dropping in the *Survey of English Dialects* (*SED*), and until fairly recently, it was the case that only the Norwich urban area showed patterns of H-Dropping, where it functioned as a clear class marker, being avoided in middle-class speech, and variably adopted in working-class speech (Trudgill 1974). More recently, however, speakers from a wider geographical area in East Anglia have adopted this innovation. Unlike the development in the TRAP set, the change in the geographical spread of H-Dropping made the accents of East Anglia more like those of other areas of England (a process known as convergence), or at least did so for a time. Somewhat confounding the efforts of the East Anglians to converge with other southern British English varieties, many speakers in the south-east are abandoning H-Dropping: evidence from Milton Keynes and Reading (Williams and Kerswill 1999), and particularly from ethnic minority groups in working-class areas of inner London, suggests that (h):[h] variants are more frequently attested in contemporary urban southern British English.

A further example of convergence is the spread of Standard English morphosyntactic forms across the British Isles. Looking at the results of the *SED*, we see that forms like *een, shoon* and *kine* for 'eyes', 'shoes' and 'cows' were once well attested in northern varieties, while the use of *her* as the subject of a sentence (as in *her is my wife*) could be found in south-western varieties. Such morphosyntactic features have undergone standardisation, such that fewer and fewer speakers use these forms. The *-n* plural suffix (which is maintained in the Standard English plurals *oxen* and *children*) was once a more productive suffix of English, but has been losing out to the *-s* suffix from the Old English period onwards. This kind of standardisation involves increased regularity (fewer words are marked as plural using patterns other than the *-s* inflection). By contrast, the loss of *her* as a subject pronoun increases the morphological complexity of the system: instead of having *her* as the pronoun for female referents in all syntactic positions, there is now a particular pronoun to mark the grammatical subject (that is, *she*). But both changes involve the loss of marked features, because they are either atypical or infrequent formally, regionally or socially.

Notice that there are therefore two ways in which variants associated with a larger number of varieties may infiltrate the speech of language users in a particular dialect area. One type of exogenous change involves the adoption of standard forms, the kind of variants that will typically be used in careful style or by middle-class people, or be associated with the written language (in the case of morphosyntactic patterns, or lexical choices). The other type of exogenous change involves the adoption of widespread non-standard forms. We might think that the consequence of this will be that a new, general, non-standard variety of British English emerges, but in fact this is not the case. It is true that particular features have a wide currency among varieties of British English (features like H-Dropping as noted above, and also TH-Fronting and T-Glottaling); but this has to be seen alongside other features which make a variety distinctive.

An associated issue concerns the way in which linguistic variation correlates with a speaker's attempt to mark a particular kind of social identity. Recall that this issue was discussed in relation to recent analyses of stylistic variation in Chapter 4. In that chapter, we said that speakers may choose from a set of variants of a given variable in order to mark allegiance with a particular social group (which in turn may simultaneously be associated with a particular region). But it is not simply the variants which mark identity; the variables themselves may function as identity markers. By this I mean that the very adoption of variability may be used to signal some sort of social identity. If a speaker from a town near Norwich in East Anglia begins to use variable (h), then it is not simply the presence or absence of [h], but the fact that there is even variation in the first place, that may go some way to characterise a particular identity.

Before we go on to look in detail at particular instances of dialect contact, there is one other issue to be addressed, which again is associated with identity, and the distinctiveness of a particular variety. In a study of New Zealand English, Meyerhoff and Niedzielski (2003) examined the distribution of a set of phonological and lexical features which have recently appeared in New Zealand English and seem to have been 'borrowed' from American English. For example, some New Zealanders pronounce *better* as [bɛɾə], with an alveolar tap as the intervocalic consonant; or they may use the word *hood* instead of *bonnet*, when talking about a particular part of a car. While this is certainly evidence of divergence (an increase in variation in New Zealand English), it is less clear that this is perceived by New Zealanders to be the adoption of a set of Americanisms (and thus reflecting the influence, or the globalisation, of American English) – they may simply see this as a new feature of vernacular New Zealand English. If this is the case, "these forms are not part of a more self-conscious alignment with a non-New Zealand identity, but rather, they are part of the variety a speaker may use in those very contexts when one is least mindful of one's speech" (Meyerhoff and Niedzielski 2003: 547). This has important ramifications for other aspects of the influence of one variety on another. If a Californian uses the word *wee* for 'little', it is not necessarily the case that they are attempting to project some sort of 'Scottish' identity; and if a Scotsman uses [f] instead of [θ] in words like *tooth*, he is not necessarily trying to sound like a Londoner. Rather, the adoption of such innovation increases the range of variants which – at a local, rather than a global level – may have correlations with particular kinds of identity. But this identity is created locally, not globally.

We can now consider particular cases of dialect contact, and the linguistic outcomes involved. One salient feature that distinguishes speakers from the north of England from those in the south concerns the vowel in words like *put* and *putt*. Northerners have the same vowel in the words *put* and *putt* (/ʊ/ in both), while southerners have two different vowels, /ʊ/ for *put*, and /ʌ/ for *putt*. This is the result of an earlier change known as the FOOT/STRUT split, using terms of the lexical sets of Wells (1982). But there comes a point where north and south meet, and the question arises as to the phonological system of the speakers of this area, who are likely to be in frequent contact with both 'northern' speakers and 'southern' speakers: are speakers at the heart of this dialect contact area all linguistically either northerners or southerners, or is there some sort of 'compromise' variety that emerges?

When we consult the *SED* to explore what was found when field-workers visited the area in the mid-twentieth century, we discover that not only did some speakers have a northern system, some a southern system, and some a 'compromise' system, but that those in the last group compromised in different ways (Chambers and Trudgill 1998: 106–13). Some had a mixed system ([ʊ] in some STRUT words, like northerners, but a few STRUT words with [ʌ], like southerners); some had a fudged system (neither [ʊ] nor [ʌ] in STRUT words, but rather [ɤ], a variant that shares some features of [ʊ] and some of [ʌ]); and some had a mixed, fudged system ([ʊ], [ʌ] and [ɤ] in various words in the STRUT set). These speakers are therefore very creative in negotiating the differences between the accents that surround them, accommodating to their neighbours in very sophisticated ways. The system in this transition zone between the two dialect areas shows a complex pattern of distribution of old and new forms.

The phenomenon described is one which has emerged as a result of long-term accommodation over an extended period of time, and the data we have are collected typically from the NORMs described in Chapter 4, so contact between speakers in these communities might have been fairly infrequent (remember that they were typically 'non-mobile'). Some sociolinguists have been concerned with exploring patterns which may be associated with dialect contact in urban communities. In Tyneside English, for instance, the vowel in the FACE set has been undergoing some significant changes. A recent survey (see Watt and Milroy 1999 for further details) showed a number of variants for this vocalic variable in the speech of a group of Tynesiders, ranging from the highly localised (for example, [fɪəs] 'face') to an RP-like variant (for example, [feɪs]). These two variants mark extremes on a continuum from the highly local to the highly supra-local; what's more, it was clear that few speakers really favoured either extreme. The most localised form was sometimes used by male speakers (young and old, middle- and working-class, but most typical of the older working class), and only very rarely by the female informants. By contrast, the RP variant was generally very rare across the entire group. Instead of moving towards either extreme, the change in Tyneside seems to be more towards a 'general' northern form, something like [feːs] for *face*. There may be a number of possible motivations for this change, but one feature which may be relevant is the relationship between language and identity. Using highly localised features may be seen to mark a strong affinity with local norms and values, and it seems to be the case that some speakers from 'traditional' urban English dialect areas are seeking to project a slightly different identity through the choice of particular linguistic forms. In other words, by rejecting highly localised forms, and by not adopting high-prestige forms associated with a very particular social category, speakers are able to negotiate a position which still marks them as 'generally northern'.

So far we have been discussing the outcome of contact in British dialects in communities which have been established for a considerable period of time. What happens when socially and geographically mobile speakers come into contact in a new community? And more importantly, what kind of accent do children born into such a community have? In order to answer this question, we need to find an example of a community which is newly created.

One example of such a community is the new town (the product of a government development programme which sets up an urban area in a previously rural community). Milton Keynes in southern England is such a new town, and has been the site of substantial sociolinguistic fieldwork (see Williams and Kerswill 1999 and references therein). The town has a large proportion of residents from southern England (particularly from London), and others from elsewhere in the UK and the rest of the world. Linguistic variation in new towns is of particular interest to sociolinguists, because of the special demographics of such communities. For many individuals, particular life changes may correlate with disruption to and reorganisation of the social networks to which the individual belongs. For instance, going to a new school, or coming to university, involves the creation of new friendship networks, and the negotiation of power relations with new individuals. In such cases, these regroupings take place within a context of established networks (for example, where older children at school already have established friendship groups). The creation of a new town involves much more substantial restructuring, because there are few existing groups in the new community at the point of its creation. Furthermore, many of the residents of the new town are (by definition) geographically mobile, and possibly also socially mobile; and as we saw in Chapter 5, increased social and geographic mobility can give rise to linguistic change. This contrasts with the kind of linguistic stability we see in certain sectors of established urban communities, where strong networks typically inhibit changes. In other words, we see a parallel between social heterogeneity and linguistic heterogeneity: the more varied the social 'make-up' of the community is, the more diverse the set of linguistic forms will be, at least initially.

Research into accent variation in Milton Keynes has shown this to be the case. Table 8.1 shows variation in the vowel of the MOUTH lexical set.

These data provide us with a great deal of information regarding the linguistic patterns associated with new dialect formation:

Table 8.1 MOUTH in Milton Keynes and surrounding villages (adapted from Kerswill 2002: 697, table 26.9).

	[ɛʊ]	[ɛɪ]	[ɛː]	[aː]	[æʊ]	[aʊ]
SED	100	–	–	–	–	–
Elderly	63.2	25.6	9.8	0	1.2	0
Women age 25–40	0	0	11.7	17.2	38.6	31.5
Girls age 14	0	0	0	5.9	4.7	88.8
Boys age 14	0	0	0	12.3	3.8	83.1

- The existing 'local' variant is not adopted. The second column in Table 8.1 shows the proportion of the [ɛʊ] variant in the recordings. This is the variant that the traditional dialectological survey, the *SED*, found to be typical in the area. Note that this feature is the one that is favoured by the 'elderly' group (this is a group of speakers who had lived in small villages and towns that now form part of the larger Milton Keynes conurbation). However, neither the women age 25–40, who had moved to Milton Keynes from other parts of the country (and indeed, other parts of the world), nor their children, used this form at all.

- The set of variants which characterise the women's language is more evenly distributed than is the case with either the elderly speakers or the children. Indeed, not all of the variants produced by the children's caregivers are provided here: there were some caregivers from Scotland who had a monophthongal [ʉ] in some instances, a further indication of the diffuse nature of the caregivers' language with respect to this particular variable. Elderly speakers clearly favour the local, traditional form; children, by contrast, are favouring a different variant [aʊ] that is not imbued with any particular social meaning (in part by virtue of being non-local; see further Kerswill et al. 2008). So across the age range, we move from focused (elderly) to diffuse (caregivers) then back to focused (children), but with a change in which particular variant the groups focus on.

What has been described here is sometimes called koineisation; it is important to distinguish this both from dialect levelling and from geographical diffusion, though all three are connected to patterns of long-term accommodation. First, dialect levelling has been defined as "a process whereby differences between regional varieties are reduced, features which make varieties distinctive disappear, and new features emerge and are adopted by speakers over a wide geographical area"

(Williams and Kerswill 1999: 149). However, as Watson (2006) observes, it is helpful to separate out geographical diffusion (the spread of new linguistic features from one urban community to the next, or from an urban community into the surrounding rural community, as discussed in Chapter 4) from levelling, a reduction in phonologically marked variants. The term 'markedness' may refer to linguistic or social features – for example, one aspect of a linguistically 'marked' feature in English is a diphthongal vocalic variant with a rounded second element (for example, [əʏ]), while one kind of socially marked variant is one that is associated with a highly localised group (for example, a variant that is characteristic of the local rural community in a new town setting, or a variant associated with traditional lower-working-class speakers in an established urban community). Both linguistically and socially marked variants are typically disfavoured in situations of dialect contact; however, it is not always the case that marked variants disappear. For instance, despite the fact that [əʏ] is a phonologically marked form in English, there is actually some evidence of the spread of this feature in outer London female speech, though it is rarer in inner London communities (Kerswill et al. 2008).

In terms of dialects in England, then, Kerswill's research has shown that many of the features associated with careful, middle-class, southeastern speech (which we typically associate with the spoken Standard English of England) have permeated across the UK, with the result that many parts of the UK are now very similar in terms of dialect (particularly in terms of lexical and grammatical variation). However, some features of the accent (that is, the phonetic and phonological variation) have not in fact spread beyond the south-east: in these cases, what we see are patterns of local convergence, associated with major urban centres like Manchester and Glasgow.

8.3 Dialect contact beyond Britain

A very interesting intersection between modern sociolinguistics and studies in the history of English concerns the development of English in 'new' communities overseas. The spread of English around the world provides some useful data for testing some of the claims associated with contemporary dialect contact and levelling. We still need to bear in mind the issues associated with doing historical sociolinguistics (see Chapter 6), but it is nevertheless useful to see whether the same kinds of patterns (for example, initial diffuseness in early contact, followed by levelling and focusing in the subsequent generation of new dialect acquirers) seem to emerge from the historical data.

One way of trying to ascertain this is to look at informal observations made by visitors to the new settlements. Some of the comments made by observers of American English in the colonial and early post-colonial period reflect not only some interesting attitudes towards the languages and dialects spoken in different communities, but also provide some anecdotal evidence in support of the claim that dialect contact was a factor in the development of the new varieties. For instance, the three observations below suggest that late eighteenth- and early nineteenth-century American English is characterised by more levelled varieties than is the case with British dialects:

(1) it is agreed, that there is greater uniformity of dialect throughout the United States (in consequence of the frequent removals of people from one part of our country to another) than is to be found throughout England. (Pickering 1816: 11)

(2) In England, almost every county is distinguished by a peculiar dialect; even different habits, and different modes of thinking, evidently discriminate inhabitants, whose local situation is not far remote: but in Maryland, and throughout adjacent provinces, it is worthy of observation, that a striking similarity of speech universally prevails . . . The colonists are composed of adventurers, not only from every district of Great Britain and Ireland, but from almost every other European government, where the principles of liberty and commerce have operated with spirit and efficacy. Is it not, therefore, reasonable to suppose, that the English language must be greatly corrupted by such a strange intermixture of various nations? The reverse, however, is true. The language of the immediate descendants of such a promiscuous ancestry is perfectly uniform, and unadulterated. (William Eddis, Letter, 1770, cited in Carver 1992: 136)

(3) I ought perhaps to except [from the universal prevalence of dialect] the United States of America, in which dialect is hardly known; unless some scanty remains of the croaking, guttural idioms of the Dutch, still observable in New York; the Scotch-Irish, as it used to be called, in some of the back settlers of the Middle States; and the whining, canting drawl brought by some republican, Oliverian and Puritan emigrants from the West of England, and still kept up by their unregenerated descendants of New England – may still be called dialects. (Jonathan Boucher, 1800, cited in Montgomery 2001: 97–8)

This anecdotal evidence is useful as a general indication of some patterns, but is not really sufficient for detailed analysis of the role of contact and levelling in new dialect formation. What is needed is some fuller record of earlier speech.

One such record is the Origins of New Zealand English (ONZE) corpus, which has been used in a number of studies regarding the formation of New Zealand English (for example, Gordon et al. 2004; Trudgill 2004). This corpus contains recordings of conversations with elderly informants, the children of early settlers in New Zealand, who were recorded in the 1940s. The informants typically came from rural areas. The accents of these informants are remarkably diffuse, which as we have seen is atypical of established communities, so this suggests that such data may be of value for research into new dialect formation.

Trudgill (2004) makes some particular claims regarding the development of new dialects: specifically, he argues that the social context of dialect formation in New Zealand is somewhat different from that of Milton Keynes, because there is greater continuity with the latter than is the case with the former (see also Kerswill and Trudgill 2005 for a comparison of dialect contact in Milton Keynes and New Zealand). Trudgill goes further to suggest there is something deterministic about new dialect formation in what he describes as *tabula rasa* contexts (where there are no existing speakers of the language). This model marginalises the role of social factors in certain stages of dialect contact, and relies instead rather more on pure demographics. Knowledge of the proportion of speakers from different established dialect areas (for example, central Scotland, or southern England), and the linguistic systems associated with those dialect areas, at the time of initial contact in New Zealand, should be sufficient to predict the linguistic system of the new variety. Accommodation plays an important role for the original settlers and their descendants, as do the processes of levelling and focusing discussed above.

According to Trudgill, early contact is characterised by rudimentary levelling (where marked variants disappear, because they are socially salient, by virtue of being markers of a minority group, for instance, or being already stigmatised in British English of the period); the next stage (which is largely represented by the speech of the informants recorded as part of the ONZE project) is one of significant diffuseness, at the level both of the individual speaker, and of the group. This is because factors like prestige do not exert influence in these circumstances, because the variants are not socially stratified in a meaningful way: there are no social motivations for dialect acquirers to select any one variant instead of any other, so a wide range of variants is likely to characterise the accent of these informants. The only factor which is likely to be of importance is pure frequency, which itself is of relevance to the focused variety which emerges in the third stage. Those variants which occur most frequently are likely to 'win out' in the focused variety. A rather different account is provided by Gordon et al. (2004), who argue more strongly for social factors in the emergence of New Zealand English. They suggest that New Zealand was not really a *tabula rasa*, or at least not for long, since more urban settlements quickly developed along particular ethnic (often religious) lines, and further immigration from Britain led to more salient social groupings which would favour the development of socially marked, and possibly even prestige, variants. Certainly, educational policy may well have established the promotion of particular forms as socially more appropriate.

Comparing patterns in Milton Keynes and New Zealand may develop our understanding of the role of dialect contact in linguistic change, but the socioeconomic situation is rather different in each case – not least because the Milton Keynes data detail the creation of an urban variety, while the ONZE data represent rural varieties. Certainly there is considerable room for debate regarding the role of social factors in new dialect formation. With this in mind, the final section of this chapter concerns the role of networks in dialect contact.

8.4 Networks and dialect contact

One interesting way to correlate patterns associated with dialect contact and levelling with more general sociolinguistic principles is to return to our notion of the social network (see Chapters 2, 4 and 5). When we consider the social processes underlying many of our dialect contact scenarios, we can observe that one common link to them all is increased mobility. Whether this concerns contemporary societies (where people move into new towns, or are increasingly commuting over larger areas, and into urban centres, for employment) or earlier communities (where people moved across the globe to settle in new lands), what we see are social networks where early ties may be broken, and new ones established: a change in the density and plexity of the network links, and potentially of the members of the individual's network. In Chapters 4 and 5, we saw that the continuation of strong network links in local areas tends to preserve the vernacular, while disruption to networks may result in increased standardisation. In situations of dialect levelling, we might suggest that the loss of the heavily localised forms may be related to the disruption of heavily localised strong network bonds; yet the emergence of regional standards suggests that some strong sense of identity is maintained across the region. This results in a complex layering of degrees of localness, all bound up with attempts to project a kind of identity: not too local to seem 'small town', but not too general to have lost any indications of where a speaker comes from.

We can try to link this issue of identity to different kinds of linguistic variables too. For instance, research on some morphosyntactic variation seems to suggest that this has become much more homogeneous over time; levelling and standardisation seem to have affected grammatical variables more readily than they have affected the phonological or phonetic ones. In Milton Keynes, for instance, researchers found little evidence of local grammatical variation among younger speakers. This did not mean that they were all using Standard English all of the time; rather, it meant that the speakers typically used supra-local non-standard forms (Cheshire et al. 2005). Turning to accent variables, it seems to be the case that consonantal variation (in British English at least) tends to be used less as a way of marking local identity than vocalic variation does (see Chapter 4). Many consonantal variants have a large geographical spread across the United Kingdom, while vocalic variants continue to be used as a 'badge' of localness.

8.5 Summary

How are we to explain the different kinds of reduction in variation that affect (a) different kinds of variables and (b) different communities? The decrease in morphosyntactic variation may be partly associated with increased dialect contact that comes with increased geographical mobility, but it is also strongly associated with social mobility, particularly as more and more people become educated, and for a longer period of time, so more people are exposed more often (and for longer) to the standard dialect in formal education. Accent variation is more complex still. While some evidence from adult language may suggest that accommodation to middle-class norms is of relevance to more homogeneous language in older speakers, patterns associated with younger dialect users require additional explanations. It seems to be the case, however, that studies of dialect contact illustrate nicely the relationship between linguistic variation and the social characteristics of the speakers in a given area: in situations of great social diversity (for example, after periods of initial contact), where the speech community is more heterogeneous, we see a corresponding diffuseness in the set of linguistic forms; as that community begins to cohere, we see a reduction in variation, associated with increased levelling and standardisation.

Exercise

Study the data in Figure 8.1, then answer the questions that follow. These data show the distribution of TH-Fronting in Glasgow. Note

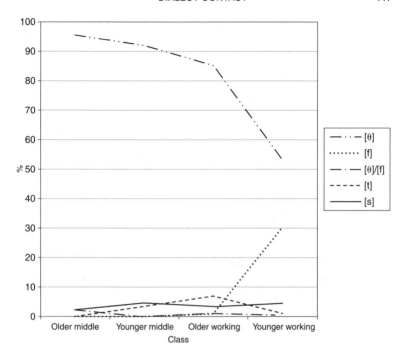

Figure 8.1 TH-Fronting in Glasgow (Stuart-Smith and Timmins 2007: 236).

Note: Word list style only; scores for [h] (0 per cent for all groups) and [m] (2.27 per cent for older working class, 0 per cent for all other groups) not represented.

that the figure is an adapted and simplified version of the data presented in Table 5 of Stuart-Smith and Timmins (2007: 236), because (a) only data from the word list style have been used and (b) two variants have not been included in the graph, for ease of visual representation. These variants are [h] and [m]; there were no instances of [h] in word list style for any groups; for [m] there was a score of 2.27 among the older working classes. It is always very important, when describing variation, to ensure that all the variants of a given variable are recorded and reported (part of what Labov 1972 describes as the principle of accountability). The variant [θ]/[f] is described by the authors as being phonetically intermediate between labial and dental fricatives.

    a. Describe the distribution of variants of (θ) in Glasgow in this particular speech style.

b. Based on what has been said about TH-Fronting elsewhere in Britain (see index for the relevant pages), does this development in Glasgow appear to be an instance of convergence to other non-standard accents in the UK, or divergence? On what grounds have you made this decision?

c. From these data, who appears to be leading the change? Is this typical or atypical for this kind of change?

d. What other evidence would be useful in explaining the social and discourse context of TH-Fronting in Glasgow?

Further reading

Trudgill (1986) is an early monograph on dialect contact, and some of the views expressed there are revised in Trudgill (2004). Dialect levelling and dialect contact are explored using data from British English by Watt and Milroy (1999) and Williams and Kerswill (1999). Kerswill (2002) provides a comprehensive summary of accommodation and koineisation, using data from a range of languages. Britain (2006) provides a very helpful summary of central issues in contact linguistics, discussing both dialect and language contact.

9 Sociolinguistics and linguistic theory

9.1 Overview

This ninth chapter is concerned with the place of sociolinguistics within the larger context of linguistic theory. Specifically, we will consider whether some of the findings discussed in the previous chapters are relevant to discussions about the structure of language. If they are, we will also need to consider how best to incorporate such findings into theoretical accounts of language.

In Chapter 1, we considered the notion of English as a social concept, and we saw that in some ways, the term 'English' is used in social and political discourse about language as if it were a linguistic entity – that there exist sets of sounds, words and clauses which make up the English language. This view has been adopted by individuals and groups who have attempted to plan English, as we saw in Chapter 3. We have also seen that for some sociolinguists, what makes something 'English' is whatever a community of speakers who claim to speak English believe to be 'English'. Taking both of these views into account, English is therefore a linguistic system which operates as a communal property, owned and policed in different ways at different levels of the community for different purposes. It may be used at the level of government to promote a particular national policy, and it may be used at the level of local community to mark a group identity. In terms of a system, we can suggest that what defines a community grammar of English is a tacit agreement on a series of shared norms, which explains, in the case of stable sociolinguistic variables, the regular distribution of variants across different social groups in different speech styles.

We have also, however, noted that not all linguists (including some sociolinguists) agree with this account. First, we have seen that it must be the case that any individual who claims to speak English does not in fact have command of all of the linguistic resources which could possibly be construed as English. At a trivial level, this can be exemplified by lexical knowledge: no individual knows all of the words of English; they only know a subset of these words. This holds true not only for lexical knowledge, but also for phonological and syntactic knowledge. Thus (1) below is perfectly well formed for some speakers of English in India:

(1) What he is doing?

but would not be considered as well formed for many speakers of English in other countries. This in itself is not a problem for a community grammar account: we can simply state that the norms for speakers of vernacular Indian English regarding *wh-* question formation are different from those of speakers of other varieties. But this issue of dialect variation is critical for an account of language structure, not just in terms of what it says about broad dialect areas, but also in terms of what it tells us about individual linguistic knowledge. This is relevant because, as we have seen, variation is an integral part of the linguistic knowledge of an individual: our discussion of the linguistic variable has shown that speakers regularly make use of alternative ways of communicating a particular message in order to affiliate themselves to a particular group, or to project a particular kind of identity. This links to some research in quantitative sociolinguistics which has attempted to understand 'how variables mean', and how this relates to identity. A speaker from the north-east of Scotland who uses (2a) in one speech act and (2b) in another has command of both variants, and can exploit this knowledge to signal a range of different social characteristics:

(2a) I don't know him.
(2b) I na ken him.

The linguistic variation here is phonological, lexical and morphosyntactic. What does it tell us about the place of such variation in terms of linguistic structure? And how does this relate to the fact that the social context of the speech act, and the social characteristics of the speaker and addressee, may influence which of the forms is uttered on any particular occasion? Is it possible to bring together some of the findings of 'biolinguistics' (the subdiscipline of linguistics which is concerned with the mental representations of phonological and syntactic structures) and 'sociolinguistics' (Cornips and Corrigan 2005), and what (if any) contribution can this make to our understanding of English? Is there a significant difference between the mental grammar and language use? These are the questions we will be seeking to address in this chapter.

9.2 The relationship between biolinguistics and sociolinguistics

Biolinguistic inquiry and sociolinguistic inquiry in the second half of the twentieth century were practically always treated as two separate intellectual domains, with very little research which attempted to bring the two together in a systematic way. Some biolinguists were concerned about the "theoretical pretentions" (Chomsky 1979: 55) of sociolinguistics, and believed that variationist sociolinguistics provided "nothing of interest to linguistic theory" (Smith 1989: 180). Similarly, some sociolinguists argued that many of the specific axioms of generative linguistics were of little use to the variationist enterprise, because such axioms were constantly being proposed, tested and then rejected (Chambers 2003).

Not all linguists have taken such diametrically opposed views on biolinguistics and sociolinguistics. Hudson (1986, 1997) takes an approach which attempts to offer the best of both worlds, by incorporating sociolinguistic data into a specific (cognitive, 'prototype') model of language structure. His concept of language structure is radically different to what some other models have invoked to explain patterns of variation in various speech communities, as Hudson notes: for instance, Guy (1994) examines alternation between the presence and absence of the alveolar oral stops word-finally where they follow another consonant (as in *guest/guessed* and *bold/bowled*) within a framework of Lexical Phonology, while Kroch (1994) considers the development of *do*-periphrasis (and the concomitant changes involving 'verb raising') in early Modern English using a particular formal apparatus. While there may be no consensus on which theoretical model of language structure is best suited to incorporating and explaining variable data, Hudson, Guy and Kroch do at least seem to agree that there is a real need to synthesise the findings of sociolinguistic investigations with aspects of theoretical linguistics. A critical question, however, remains: can the findings of sociolinguistic inquiry be directly incorporated into a particular biolinguistic model of language structure (so that there is a genuine synthesis of the two subdisciplines), or are the two subdisciplines distinct, but linked in a "mutually supportive" (Chomsky 2001: 41) way?

9.3 What do speakers know?

One of the clearest findings of sociolinguistics is that speakers command a knowledge of variation, which manifests itself in the use of variables, giving rise to particular varieties. Sometimes those varieties are considered to be languages, in which case we speak of 'multilinguals';

but even in the case of 'monolinguals', such speakers display regular stylistic shifts between more standard and more vernacular forms of the language. We have seen that such linguistic differences can be exploited by speakers to negotiate aspects of their identity, to project a particular aspect of their social persona, or to accommodate to other participants in the discourse. The last of these was shown to be highly influential in situations of language and dialect contact (Chapters 7 and 8).

We saw in Chapter 4 that the concept of the linguistic variable has been a most important one for our understanding of sociolinguistic variation. The sociolinguistic variable has been defined as "a set of alternative ways of saying the same thing, although the alternatives will have social significance" (Fasold 1990: 223–4). Essentially what this means is that the variants of a variable all have semantic equivalence: whether I say *pity* with an intervocalic tap or a glottal stop is irrelevant to the semantics of the word; the nouns *spanner* and *wrench* can both refer to the same entity; and *the man who died*, *the man that died* and *the man as died* are all noun phrases with the same referential meaning, even though the form of the relative pronoun differs in each case. However, the use of one variant over another may index a series of stylistic, social and regional characteristics.

All of these examples, however, have been concerned with particular kinds of variable (phonetic, lexical and morphosyntactic). Far more problematic for our purposes is the syntactic variable. We will begin with a fairly standard example, the agentless passive, and then move on to another, more complex pattern.

A passive clause is one which is marked by a change in the relation between grammatical roles (such as subject and object) and semantic roles (such as agent, the source of the action, and patient, the thing that is acted upon) in comparison with the active counterpart of the passive clause. Compare, for example, the active clause (3) and its passive counterpart (4):

(3) My friend has kissed my sister.
(4) My sister has been kissed by my friend.

In the passive version (4), *my sister* has become the subject and *my friend* is now the complement of a preposition: but crucially, the semantic roles have remained constant – my sister is still the patient, the entity that is acted upon (in other words, still the thing that is kissed), and my friend is still the agent, the source of the action. So when an active clause becomes a passive clause, the grammatical roles change, but the semantic roles remain the same.

It is also possible to form a passive without mentioning the agent:

(5) My sister has been kissed.

The corresponding active form of (5) would be something like:

(6) Someone kissed my sister.

Now the question is whether (5) and (6) are variants of the same variable. The problem is that with syntactic variables, we are really dealing with the interface between syntax and discourse, pragmatics or semantics (that is, some kind of meaning). One of the functions associated with passive constructions is concerned with thematic ordering: by moving the patient into subject position, we may give it greater discourse prominence, or we may signal to the hearer that it is the topic of the utterance. As soon as such discourse issues come in to play, we have to question whether or not the two variants really mean the same thing.

The second example concerns a phenomenon called right-node raising (RNR), mentioned in Chapter 2 (see Moore 2004). Examples of RNR are:

(7) He$_i$'s a funny man, Mr Jones$_i$.
(8) That$_i$'s just stupid, that$_i$.

The subscript i in examples (7) and (8) indicates co-referentiality (e.g. *he* and *Mr Jones* in (7) refer to the same person). Again, as with the passive, with RNR we see the interface between syntax and discourse. RNR is a discourse strategy that speakers of English use to clarify the reference of a preceding (or anaphoric) pronoun, as in (7). Speakers may still use this pattern to mark identity – it may well be imbued with social meaning – but it is more difficult in cases such as these to suggest that there are genuine variants of one particular variable, because it is by no means clear that alternative construals unambiguously mean the same thing.

With truly syntactic variation, therefore, we may need to recognise that the syntactic variable is ontologically different from all other kinds of linguistic variable (including the morphosyntactic variable, which is discussed in some detail in the following sections).

9.4 The problem of Standard English and dialect syntax

In Chapters 3 and 6, we considered the rise of Standard English as part of a survey of language planning and English historical sociolinguistics.

In those chapters, the notion of Standard English was shown to be a problematic one, partly because the term has a range of different applications. It can sometimes be used to describe a codified, planned variety of English (often associated with the written language) that is alleged to have a cross-cultural application – it is the variety that is taught in schools, the variety that is held up as a model of 'good' usage to learners of English as a second or other language (as well as to non-standard speakers of English as a first language), the variety of serious discourse. But Standard English has also had a central role to play in the development of linguistic theories.

One effect of Standard English on the development of linguistic theories has been in the nature of the data used to construct and test the various principles or axioms that go to make up an individual model. Most of the work in theoretical linguistics uses data that are based on speaker judgements: the linguist will ask someone (most often, himself) whether a given linguistic string is grammatical or not. Because the theorist is interested primarily in the biological, genetic language faculty that manifests itself slightly differently in different people, he will normally adopt what is known as an (internalised) I-language approach (Chomsky 1986), which is purely concerned with constraints on well-formed utterances (and the reasons for ill-formedness). Here language is treated as a purely mental object: an I-language is the internal mental system which defines a speaker's knowledge of language. The influence of the standard is felt here in one of two ways: first, if the data gathering is entirely introspective, the model is likely to be built around a data set which approximates closely to Standard English, since most academic linguists will have been educated to such a degree that their language will be standard; second, even if other speakers are asked to provide judgements, the effects of the standard – given its association with appropriate or 'good' English – can distort a speaker's responses. In addition, what a speaker says and what a speaker does are not always the same thing: a speaker may therefore consider a particular construction to be ill formed, while at the same time using it quite happily in specific discourse contexts. Research on dialect grammar within any given theoretical framework therefore raises the very important issue of what the framework is actually attempting to account for.

9.5 (Socio)linguistic modelling

As Adger and Trousdale (2007) point out, syntactic theories tend to build on standard data, with some lip service paid to variation. This has sometimes been justified on the grounds that Standard English, unlike native speaker intuitions, is a social object, not a natural one, which itself is a debatable point, not least because there are some speakers whose idiolect can be identified with the standard variety. None the less, introspective data are similarly typically based on the idiolect of a highly educated speaker, that is, one who has been exposed over a long time to the standard variety; it is therefore possible that grammaticality intuitions for such speakers may not be the direct manifestation of an I-language, but one which has been passed through the Standard English filter. Moreover, much of the theory is built around standard written English, rather than spoken data. Bybee (2006) has also observed that using a corpus of texts, and making generalisations about externalised language (the E-language perspective as defined by Chomsky 1986) helps to correct some of the possible biases inherent in using solely introspection as a guide to well-formedness. The question is whether (and if so, how) we should bridge the gap between I-language and E-language for a proper understanding of the nature of variation, its mental representation, and its social correlates.

For instance, imagine a researcher who has collected a corpus of data over a period of time, having adopted an ethnographic method, and has analysed the data, establishing (via the use of a statistical program) whether the variation correlates with linguistic constraints, social constraints or both. The question then arises as to what is actually being modelled:

a. the corpus alone (that is, the set of utterances which has made up a corpus), which we can classify as the E-language approach;
b. the biological, genetic language faculty which generates the structures underlying such utterances, which we can classify as the I-language approach;
c. the language of the community of speakers, and the social factors relevant to the context of production of the utterances, which we can classify, using terminology adopted in ongoing work by David Adger and Jennifer Smith, as an S-language approach.

Much syntactic theorising has been based on the intuitions of the native speaker, as a reflection of a particular I-language. By contrast, much sociolinguistic research is concerned with E-language and with S-language, largely as a result of the widespread belief among sociolinguists in a community grammar (based largely on the notion of conventionalisation). The problem is how to link E- and S-grammars to I-grammars. Some linguists have argued that this is not possible: "There is no way that one can draw conclusions about the grammar of an individual from usage facts about communities" (Newmeyer 2003: 696). Others are less pessimistic.

For Adger and Trousdale (2007: 271), "[t]he reason why people who live closely together can understand each other is because they share a genetic endowment (by virtue of being human) and common (linguistic) experience. However . . . everyone's experience is slightly different, and so we expect to see very small variations between the I-languages of people who, in commonsense terms, speak the same dialect". Note that there is nothing here that claims that community grammars exist, and what is stated here is just as applicable to a network-based model of language and society (see Hudson 1996). The undoubted sense of a community which correlates with linguistic variation may be based not on shared norms in the sense of Labov (1972), but rather on social practices and the creation of social identity (Eckert 2000; Moore 2004).

9.6 The modular approach

One way in which researchers have tried to incorporate sociolinguistics into a formal linguistic theory is to divide up what speakers know about language into a grammar component and a usage component (Adger 2006). The grammar component is uniquely linguistic: that is, there is no social information encoded in the grammatical representation. For instance, imagine a speaker who varies between saying *he was reading* and *he were reading*. These data suggest that the speaker has two variants of a morphosyntactic variable, which we can call (BE past): *was* and (BE past): *were*. Speakers of Standard English use both *was* and *were* too, of course, but this is not variable if the subject of the clause is held constant: that is, Standard English speakers always use *was* with first person singular (*I*) and third person singular (for example, *he, she* or *it*) subjects, and always use *were* with any other subject. The difference between this and some non-standard dialects is that the non-standard speaker can vary between *I was reading* and *I were reading*, or *he was reading* and *he were reading*, a variation not available to the Standard English speaker.

In the modular model, the grammar produces these variants, resulting in a set of forms which may be selected in a given usage event, in a way akin to whether or not a given lexical variant is selected. In other words, in this model, there is only one major difference between the variants in (9) and the variants in (10):

(9)   (BE past): *was* ~ *were*
(10) ('multi-seat piece of furniture'): *sofa* ~ *couch*

The difference is that the variants in the first set are generated by the grammar, and those in the second set are stored in the lexicon. But once variants are produced by the grammar, the speaker can select a particular 'grammatical' variant in the same way as he can select a 'lexical' variant. Just as the choice of *sofa* over *couch* may correlate with the group membership of the speaker, or the speaker's style, so the choice of *I was* over *I were* may correlate with various social and stylistic factors. Morphosyntactic variation reduces to a matter of lexical choice, except the choice here concerns functional items (that is, markers of grammatical categories like tense, aspect or voice). The critical issue is that grammatical knowledge is kept distinct from social knowledge: the system itself is very different from the use of the system, and all the sociolinguistic information about an item (whether it be a functional item like *was* or a lexical item like *sofa*) is a matter of use. This modular model also supports the notion of a community grammar, since it would suggest that the constraints on the system manifest themselves in a set of shared norms across the local community.

9.7 The usage-based model

The I-language/E-language model outlined above argues for a very sharp distinction between grammar (a biological property of the human species) and usage (the application of that system for specific communicative and social purposes). In such a theory, basic linguistic structure is hardwired in your brain at birth (as part of the human genome), and as you are exposed to language as a child, you learn specific constraints based on the input you receive, from your parents and others. So, for example, a child brought up in an English-speaking environment learns that English speakers don't allow inversion of subject and lexical verb when *yes/no* questions are formed:

(11) *Speak you English?

Instead, English speakers use a grammatical (tense) marker (the verb *do*), and the lexical verb remains after the subject:

(12) Do you speak English?

In a French-speaking environment, the child would learn that the subject and the lexical verb do invert:

(13) Parlez-vous anglais?
       Speak-you English?

Thus there is an innate language faculty, common to all members of the species, but manifest differently in different communities. This is the essence of the nativist argument. However, not all experts in language acquisition agree on this issue of nativism, and specifically on the idea that there is a distinct language faculty. Some researchers (including some of those who have tried to establish what makes human cognition different from that of related animals, such as apes) have argued that language is not substantially different from other cognitive abilities, and that children do not acquire language because of a separate language faculty, but because they are predisposed to do so as a result of more general cognitive structures (Tomasello 2003). This is the heart of the usage-based model of language: that a speaker's regular exposure to language in use might explain patterns of linguistic behaviour, and that language is largely constructed, rather than largely inherited. In the usage-based model, a central notion is that frequent exposure to particular forms of constructions gives those forms a special status in terms of a speaker's knowledge. Specifically, the more that a particular form is heard, the more directly accessible it is in the speaker's mind (that is, it is accessed directly). This has interesting consequences for our understanding of sociolinguistic variation.

For example, in this model, it is possible to claim that sociolinguistic knowledge is a kind of linguistic knowledge, which in turn is a kind of knowledge. If this is the case, then it is not only desirable to include facts about sociolinguistic patterns in a theory of grammar: it is essential to do so. Furthermore, the usage-based account suggests that we learn facts about language structure and facts about language use in much the same way. Notice that both sets of facts apply to the same phenomena: many speakers of British English know not only that *gas station* is a (compound) noun, but also that it is also used by Americans to mean 'petrol station'; when they acquire the new word *gas station*, they establish a link between that form and a typical user or context. We can extend this to issues associated with pronunciation and syntax. For instance, a user of language is likely to want to be able to report another person's speech: this particular function can be coded using a variety of different forms, which may change over time. From the Old English period to at least the early Modern English period it was possible to use the form *quoth*; in the contemporary language, there are many variants, including forms like *say* which have been attested for a long time, as well as more recent innovations, such as BE *like* (for example, *I'm like 'what did you say?'*), GO (*I went 'what did you say?'*), BE *all* (*he was all 'what did you say?'*), *this* BE *pro* (*this is me, this is him* etc.), and so on. Sociolinguists have found that particular variants are favoured by particular kinds of people in particular contexts, so a language user is able to identify not just what the variants mean, but what they index.

The language user is also able to abstract from such usage events to make more abstract schemas (just as variables may be said to be abstractions across a set of variants); they are also able to abstract from exposure to particular people to make abstract social schemas. Your knowledge of the concept 'Englishman' or 'New Yorker' is based in large part on your exposure to particular instances of Englishmen and New Yorkers (except in cases of stereotyping, where more abstract social schemas are created on basis of very limited knowledge). Since certain aspects of sociolinguistic research have shown how types of speaker may be associated with types of speech, a link becomes established between these type-abstractions, as much as between specific instances of use, and particular people. If you encounter a group of Englishmen who regularly use glottal stops in words like *butter*, and you encounter a group of New Yorkers who regularly use alveolar taps in the same set of words, it is cognitively much more economical for you to store that information at a more abstract level (that is, at the level of type) than repeatedly to store information about individual tokens.

This can be explored in greater detail using an example discussed elsewhere in this book. In Chapter 5, aspects of linguistic change in suburban Detroit were discussed (Eckert 1988, 1989, 2000), in which a particular variable (uh) was progressing through a series of local networks, spreading first in the language of the Burnouts, then to the language of the In-betweens, and then to the language of the Jocks. Eckert's study certainly revealed something about particular linguistic tokens, and the behaviour of individuals. But it also revealed something about the network of linguistic and social knowledge that characterises that community. Although it was possible to identify particular individual Jocks, it was also possible to generalise, and to talk about a Jock-type. Similarly, the various phonetic tokens can be subsumed under a general phonological type, the variable (uh). And just as much as linguistic variants may index particular social characteristics (recall the discussion of [t]-release and 'Britishness' in Chapter 4), the variation itself – the existence of variable (uh) – also indexes some kind of social meaning, because not all groups take part in the variation: if it was the case that all speakers of English are taking part in the variation, the change will have come to an end, since the change can spread no further. (Compare also the discussion of social meaning of variability in dialect contact in Chapter 8.) Recognising variability – and which groups of speakers take part in the variation – is also a feature of how variables mean; and this knowledge comes from exposure to instances of language use, and forms part of what speakers in that community know (that is, it is part of their cognition). This is at the heart of a usage-based, integrated approach to language and society.

9.8 What about 'English'?

An important question remains: what does this discussion about socio-linguistics and linguistic theory tell us about English? The answer is 'very little'; and the reason is that both modular approaches to variation and usage-based approaches to variation are essentially theories of individual knowledge, while any account of variation and change in English must make reference to a larger community. We can try to connect I-language data to phenomena associated with E- and S-languages, but here we encounter the same problems as we identified in Chapter 1, namely that establishing a sharp boundary around any given community is problematic. Thus when Adger writes: "every community member will have the same grammar" (Adger 2006: 527), it is important we ask how we establish whether or not someone is a member of that given community.

We saw in Chapter 1 that there is some evidence to reject the notion of English as a linguistic concept (though it is clearly a very important social concept); instead we can take as our basis the fact that individual speakers form (open-ended) social networks with one another, some parts of which are close-knit and highly influential in terms of constraining innovations. Where certain sectors of these networks involve individuals who mutually agree to come together to fulfil a specific social purpose, we often see correlations with specific linguistic practices: this is at the heart of the notion of community of practice, as we saw in Chapter 2. In such situations, speakers draw on a series of linguistic resources in order to meet the needs of the group enterprise; so the linguistic practices of the group are functional in a number of ways, particularly as a means of negotiating individual identities within a group dynamic. Note that just as in the case of social networks, communities of practice may be open-ended, with the greatest correlations between individuals and linguistic 'norms' being found at the most dense and multiplex sector of the network. As discussed above, this network model of social structure is mirrored in a network model of language structure, from which we can generalise further to say that all of cognition is a network (Hudson 2007). Part of that cognitive network is the concept 'English', which may form part of our knowledge about linguistic items. At a lower level of specification, we may associate particular linguistic forms with particular varieties (so that some individuals associate *den* with the concept 'room in a house', but also with the concept 'American'). This again has to be the product of particular usage events – you can only know that *den* is an American word for what British speakers might call *lounge* if you have been told this, or have inferred it from a conversation. Exactly the same claims can be made for phonological and morphosyntactic variation. While such information may come from direct instruction, it is typically the product of inference in conversation.

This is made even clearer in cases of language and dialect contact, discussed in Chapters 7 and 8, and in cases of language planning, discussed in Chapter 3. In cases of planning, the concept 'English' becomes explicitly, overtly linked to particular linguistic forms: we could be more specific in some contexts and talk of 'Standard English', but in some cases the distinction need not be made (since most learners of English as a second or other language do not typically learn non-standard varieties). Quite the reverse happens in cases of language contact. Here, associations between 'English' and particular linguistic forms become eroded as speakers mix languages, and create new varieties, which themselves take on new social meanings. It is possible to talk about a pidgin having English as a lexifier, but as the new variety becomes the input for acquisition among new language learners, the historic links with English become diluted – the link may be something that the linguist knows, but not the speaker. (After all, how many speakers of present-day British English would think of themselves as speaking Germanic?) And the principles we apply to language contact should hold true for dialect contact, if the claims made in Chapter 1, concerning the relationship between language and dialect, hold true. When young speakers from Glasgow use TH-Fronting, the social meaning of that variation changes – it is not associated with the social concept of 'London', but is appropriated by those speakers and given particular social meaning in that local social context (so it may index 'east end of Glasgow' or 'tough' or 'male', or a combination of these).

9.9 Summary

In this chapter we have explored some of the ways in which aspects of sociolinguistic variation in English can be explained using some aspects of theoretical linguistics. Essentially, what this research is trying to do is to investigate whether (and if so, how) facts about language use can be correlated with what we know about language as a mental system. This takes us into some very murky waters indeed (which is why it's so interesting), because such an exploration forces us to question some of the central beliefs in both sociolinguistic theory and formal linguistic theory, such as the existence of the speech community, and the idea that language is organised differently from other aspects of cognition. Some linguists have argued that the structure of language and use of language should be kept clearly distinct (for example, Newmeyer 2003); others have suggested that language structure emerges from the use of language (for example, Bybee 2006). We perhaps do not know yet which of these is the more plausible, but it is clearly a fascinating area of linguistic inquiry.

In this chapter we also explored the relevance of such research for our understanding of what 'English' is, and how we characterise varieties of English. Again, this is a highly debatable topic. Some linguists have argued for a community grammar approach, where the English language is a linguistic entity marked by agreement on shared norms; others have argued for an individual approach, based on social and cognitive networks, which suggests that English is much more of a social concept than a linguistic one (an issue which we also considered in Chapter 1). In the next chapter, which concludes this book, we will see how the many issues raised in both this chapter and the previous ones might be brought together, to see what the critical issues in English sociolinguistics might be, and to encourage you to collect and analyse your own data.

Exercise

These final questions are taxing, especially if you have no training in formal linguistics. You may find it helpful to read the final chapter of Hudson (1996) and Adger (2006) before you attempt to answer them.

1. List some of the advantages and disadvantages of incorporating non-standard data into formal accounts of language structure.

2. Illustrate the different ways in which a formal grammarian and a variationist sociolinguist might attempt to explain intra-speaker variation. How might the two traditions be brought together, in your view?

3. What are the advantages of adopting a usage-based model in an analysis of sociolinguistic variation. What are the drawbacks?

Further reading

For more on the nature of the syntactic variable, see Lavandera (1978) and Cheshire (1987); for a discussion of the relationship between dialect syntax and linguistic theory more generally, see Adger and Trousdale

(2007). The relationship between biolinguistics and sociolinguistics is discussed in the collection of papers in Cornips and Corrigan (2005): see particularly the contribution by Adger and Smith. For more on language networks and cognition, see Hudson (2007). A similar theory of sociolinguistics and language structure is discussed by Hudson in a number of other papers, particularly Hudson (1986) and Hudson (1997).

10 Conclusion

In this book, I have tried to show how studying varieties of English can be informed by the discipline of sociolinguistics. I have not attempted to cover all of what constitutes sociolinguistics; nor have I dealt with all of the ways in which English can vary. But I hope to have shown some of the ways in which English is used by individuals and communities, and how the shape of such varieties correlates with various features of the users of those varieties.

We have looked at both formal and functional variation in English; some chapters have concentrated primarily on form (on regional and social variation in English, on the sociolinguistic correlations of change in English, and on the shape of contact varieties); others have concentrated primarily on function (on the various attempts to shape and employ English in contexts of language planning, for example). But all the way through this book, we have been suggesting that the division between form and function may be somewhat arbitrary, and that sociolinguistic studies often try to explore the correlation between form and function. For example, language planning which involves English often also involves issues about which form of English to adopt; conversely, speakers who use a particular spoken form of English may be attempting to index some particular aspect of social identity, which suggests that the form selected has a particular function within any given community. This interplay between form and function is at the heart of much sociolinguistic research.

I have also tried to encourage you to think about links between contemporary societies and those in the past, and about links between societies with which you might be more familiar, and others which are likely to be more remote. Researchers of the English language are very fortunate on two fronts: one is that they have an amazing array of historical records of English to work with, to look at how the language has evolved at different times; the other is that contemporary English is used in so many diverse ways, and in so many diverse communities.

Taken together, it means we can explore English in use in a significant number of social contexts, tracking how and why it has come to have the form and function it does in so many different places on earth. I hope this book has given you a flavour of some of the things you could explore when working on English sociolinguistics.

There are some topics which have not been dealt with at all, or not in great detail, such as aspects of discourse structure, the relationships between pragmatics and politeness in English, and the relationship between developing technology and use of English. But I hope this book has provided you with a framework of ways to think about English in its social context that would allow you to plan how you might study one or more such topics, bearing in mind the critical issue of the relationship between linguistic form and linguistic function.

As you become more expert in the field of English sociolinguistics, you will realise that some of the claims made here have simplified what are very complex phenomena. And so it is important to remember that this is just the conclusion of an introduction to English sociolinguistics, and that researchers are constantly discovering new ways of analysing variation in English. Sociolinguists have a great job: they get to talk to all sorts of fascinating people in all sorts of fascinating communities, using those data to try to come to some understanding of the complex relationship between language structure and language use, how speakers use language to negotiate with their addressees, and to mark allegiances to others in very subtle ways. Some sociolinguists work on lots of different varieties, while others focus just on one. And there is no doubt that there are many questions which still need to be answered concerning the form and function of English in its social context. I hope you will enjoy trying to figure out the answers to such questions, as I do; and I hope you also enjoy coming up with new questions of your own to explore.

Appendix

List of IPA symbols with examples and a note on transcription conventions.
The International Phonetic Alphabet (IPA) is used by linguists to represent speech sounds; you can find out more at this website: http://www.langsci.ucl.ac.uk/ipa/

Below, I have given a list of some of the consonantal symbols which are most relevant for accents of English, along with an example of the word in which the sound appears (when spoken by an RP speaker of English, unless otherwise stated)

/p/ pit   /t/ tin   /k/ coal
/b/ bit   /d/ din   /g/ goal
/m/ ram   /n/ ran   /ŋ/ rang
/s/ sip   /z/ zip   /ʃ/ ship   /ʒ/ measure   /tʃ/ chinks   /dʒ/ jinx
/f/ fine   /v/ vine   /θ/ breath   /ð/ breathe
/j/ yacht   /w/ watt   /r/ rot   /l/ lot   /ʍ/ what (in conservative RP and some other varieties)
/h/ whole /x/ loch (Scottish English)

The symbol [ʔ] represents the glottal stop. This is a well-known feature of many British English accents (sometimes represented in dialect literature by an apostrophe, as in *wa'er* for 'water'). In many words which have [ʔ] between two vowels in British English accents, American, Canadian, Australian and other accents often have an alveolar tap [ɾ] (so that words like *waiter* and *wader* often sound the same in these accents).

Vowel sounds are more complex, and I have tried to use only a few examples which involve vocalic variation (some in Chapter 5, more in Chapter 8). The IPA website mentioned above has a downloadable vowel chart (http://www.langsci.ucl.ac.uk/ipa/vowels.html) which may be useful for reference. Other useful texts include the phonology textbook in this series (McMahon 2002) and (for an explanation and use of the term lexical set) Wells (1982).

Symbols enclosed in slash / / brackets in the text are phonemes, and those in square [ ] brackets are phones. As noted elsewhere in the text, variables (phonetic, morphosyntactic and lexical) are represented by curved ( ) brackets, and the variants of those variables are given after a colon. For example (t): [ʔ] represents the glottal stop variant of the variable (t).

References

Adger, David. 2006. Combinatorial variability. *Journal of Linguistics* 42: 503–30.

Adger, David and Graeme Trousdale. 2007. Variation in English syntax: Theoretical implications. *English Language and Linguistics* 11: 261–78.

Aitchison, Jean. 2001. *Language Change: Progress or Decay?* 3rd edition. Cambridge: Cambridge University Press.

Annamalai, E. 2005. Nation-building in a globalised world: Language choice and education in India. In Angel Lin and Peter Martin (eds), *Decolonisation, Globalisation: Language-in-Education Policy and Practice.* Clevedon: Multilingual Matters, 20–37.

Auer, Peter (ed.). 1998. *Code-Switching in Conversation: Language, Interaction and Identity.* London: Routledge.

Barber, Charles. 1997. *Early Modern English.* Edinburgh: Edinburgh University Press.

Bauer, Laurie. 2002. *An Introduction to International Varieties of English.* Edinburgh: Edinburgh University Press.

Beal, Joan. 2006. *Language and Region.* London: Routledge.

Bell, Allan. 1984. Language style as audience design. *Language in Society* 13: 145–204.

Bhatt, Rakesh M. 2008. In other words: Language mixing, identity representations, and *third space. Journal of Sociolinguistics* 12: 177–200.

Blommaert, Jan. 2005. Situating language rights: English and Swahili in Tanzania revisited. *Journal of Sociolinguistics* 9: 390–417.

Britain, David. 2002. Space and spatial diffusion. In J. K. Chambers, Peter Trudgill and Natalie Schilling-Estes (eds), *The Handbook of Language Variation and Change.* Oxford: Blackwell, 603–37.

Britain, David. 2006. Language/dialect contact. In Keith Brown (ed.), *Encyclopedia of Language and Linguistics.* Volume 6. 2nd edition. Oxford: Elsevier, 651–6.

Britain, David (ed.). 2007. *Language in the British Isles.* Cambridge: Cambridge University Press.

Bucholtz, Mary. 1998. Geek the girl: Language, femininity and female nerds. In Natasha Warner, Jocelyn Ahlers, Leela Bilmes, Monica Oliver, Suzanne Wertheim and Melinda Chen (eds), *Gender and Belief Systems.* Berkeley: Berkeley Women and Language Group, 119–31.

Bybee, Joan. 2006. From usage to grammar: The mind's response to repetition. *Language* 82: 711–33.

Canagarajah, A. Suresh. 2005. Dilemmas in planning English/vernacular relations in post-colonial communities. *Journal of Sociolinguistics* 9: 418–47.

Carver, Craig M. 1992. The *Mayflower* to the Model-T: The development of American English. In Tim William Machan and Charles T. Scott (eds), *English in Its Social Contexts: Essays in Historical Sociolinguistics.* Oxford: Oxford University Press, 131–54.

Cassidy, Frederic G. and Joan Houston Hall (eds). 1985–2002. *Dictionary of American Regional English.* 4 volumes. Cambridge, MA: Harvard University Press.

Chambers, J. K. 2002. Patterns of variation including change. In J. K. Chambers, Peter Trudgill and Natalie Schilling-Estes (eds), *The Handbook of Language Variation and Change.* Oxford: Blackwell, 349–72.

Chambers, J. K. 2003. *Sociolinguistic Theory: Linguistic Variation and its Social Significance.* 2nd edition. Oxford: Blackwell.

Chambers, J. K. and Peter Trudgill. 1998. *Dialectology.* 2nd edition. Cambridge: Cambridge University Press.

Chambers, J. K., Peter Trudgill and Natalie Schilling-Estes (eds). 2002. *The Handbook of Language Variation and Change.* Oxford: Blackwell.

Cheshire, Jenny. 1982. *Variation in an English Dialect.* Cambridge: Cambridge University Press.

Cheshire, Jenny. 1987. Syntactic variation, the linguistic variable, and sociolinguistic theory. *Linguistics* 25: 257–82.

Cheshire, Jenny. 2007. Discourse variation, grammaticalisation, and stuff like that. *Journal of Sociolinguistics* 11: 155–93.

Cheshire, Jenny and Viv Edwards. 1993. Sociolinguistics in the classroom: Exploring linguistic diversity. In James Milroy and Lesley Milroy (eds), *Real English: The Grammar of English Dialects in the British Isles.* London: Longman, 34–52.

Cheshire, Jenny, Paul Kerswill and Ann Williams. 2005. Phonology, grammar and discourse in dialect convergence. In Peter Auer, Frans Hinskens and Paul Kerswill (eds), *Dialect Change: Convergence and Divergence in European Languages.* Cambridge: Cambridge University Press, 135–67.

Chomsky, Noam. 1965. *Aspects of the Theory of Syntax.* Cambridge. MA: MIT Press.

Chomsky, Noam. 1979. *Language and Responsibility: Based on Conversations with Mitsou Ronat.* New York: Pantheon.

Chomsky, Noam. 1986. *Knowledge of Language: Its Nature, Origins and Use.* New York: Praeger.

Chomsky, Noam. 2001. Derivation by phase. In Michael Kenstowicz (ed.), *Ken Hale: A Life in Language.* Cambridge, MA: MIT Press, 1–52.

Coates, Jennifer. 1993. *Women, Men and Language: A Sociolinguistic Account of Gender Differences in Language.* 2nd edition. London: Longman.

Cobarrubias, Juan. 1983. Ethical issues in status planning. In Juan Cobarrubias and Joshua Fishman (eds), *Progress in Language Planning: International Perspectives*. Berlin: Mouton de Gruyter, 41–85.

Cornips, Leonie and Karen Corrigan (eds). 2005. *Syntax and Variation: Reconciling the Biological and the Social*. Amsterdam: John Benjamins.

Coulmas, Florian (ed.). 1998. *The Handbook of Sociolinguistics*. Oxford: Blackwell.

Coupland, Nikolas. 1984. Accommodation at work. *International Journal of the Sociology of Language* 46: 49–70.

Coupland, Nikolas. 2007. *Style: Language Variation and Identity*. Cambridge: Cambridge University Press.

Crystal, David. 2000. *Language Death*. Cambridge: Cambridge University Press.

Crystal, David. 2003. *English as a Global Language*. 2nd edition. Cambridge: Cambridge University Press.

Crystal, David 2006a. Into the twenty-first century. In Lynda Mugglestone (ed.), *The Oxford History of English*. Oxford: Oxford University Press, 394–413.

Crystal, David. 2006b. English worldwide. In Richard Hogg and David Denison (eds), *A History of the English Language*. Cambridge: Cambridge University Press, 420–39.

Crystal, David. 2006c. *Language and the Internet*. 2nd edition. Cambridge: Cambridge University Press.

Crystal, David. 2008. *Txting: The Gr8 Db8*. Oxford: Oxford University Press.

Cusack, Bridget. 1998. *Everyday English 1500–1700: A Reader*. Edinburgh: Edinburgh University Press.

David, Maya, and Subra Govindasamy. 2005. Negotiating a language policy for Malaysia: Local demand for affirmative action versus challenges from globalization. In A. Suresh Cangarajah (ed.), *Reclaiming the Local in Language Policy and Practice*. Mahwah, NJ: Lawrence Erlbaum, 123–45.

Davies, Alan. 2003. *The Native Speaker: Myth and Reality*. Clevedon: Multilingual Matters.

Davies, Janet. 2000. Welsh. In Glanville Price (ed.), *Languages in Britain and Ireland*. Oxford: Blackwell, 78–108.

De Fina, Anna. 2007. Code-switching and the construction of ethnic identity in a community of practice. *Language in Society* 36: 371–92.

Eckert, Penelope. 1988. Adolescent social structure and the spread of linguistic change. *Language in Society* 17: 183–207.

Eckert, Penelope. 1989. *Jocks and Burnouts: Social Categories and Identity in the High School*. New York: Teachers College Press.

Eckert, Penelope. 1990. The whole woman: Sex and gender differences in variation. *Language Variation and Change* 1: 245–67.

Eckert, Penelope. 2000. *Linguistic Variation as Social Practice: The Linguistic Construction of Identity in Belten High*. Oxford: Blackwell.

Eckert, Penelope. 2005. Variation, convention, and social meaning. Plenary paper presented at the Linguistic Society of America, Oakland CA, January 2005.

Eckert, Penelope and Sally McConnell-Ginet. 1992a. Communities of practice: Where language, gender, and power all live. In Kira Hall, Mary Bucholtz and Birch Moonwomon (eds), *Locating Power: Proceedings of the Second Berkeley Women and Language Conference*. Berkeley: Berkeley Women and Language Group, 89–99. [Reprinted in Coates, Jennifer (ed.). 1998. *Language and Gender: A Reader*. Oxford: Blackwell, 484–94.]

Eckert, Penelope and Sally McConnell-Ginet. 1992b. Think practically and look locally: Language and gender as community-based practice. *Annual Review of Anthropology* 21: 461–90.

Edwards, John R. 1982. Language attitudes and their implications among English speakers. In Ellen Bouchard Ryan and Howard Giles (eds), *Attitudes Towards Language Variation*. London: Edward Arnold, 20–33.

Fasold, Ralph. 1990. *The Sociolinguistics of Language*. Oxford: Blackwell.

Ferguson, Gibson. 2006. *Language Planning and Education*. Edinburgh: Edinburgh University Press.

Foulkes, Paul and Gerard J. Docherty (eds). 1999. *Urban Voices: Accent Studies in the British Isles*. London: Arnold.

Gordon, Elizabeth, Lyle Campbell, Jennifer Hay, Margaret Maclagan, Andrea Sudbury and Peter Trudgill. 2004. *New Zealand English: Its Origins and Evolution*. Cambridge: Cambridge University Press.

Gordon, Matthew. 2002. Investigating chain shifts and mergers. In J. K. Chambers, Peter Trudgill and Natalie Schilling-Estes (eds), *The Handbook of Language Variation and Change*. Oxford: Blackwell, 244–66.

Graddol, David. 1999. The decline of the native speaker. In David Graddol and Ulrike H. Meinhof (eds), *English in a Changing World, AILA Review* 13: 57–68.

Graddol, David. 2006. *English Next*. London: British Council.

Green, Lisa. 2002. *African American English*. Cambridge: Cambridge University Press.

Gumperz, John J. 1982. *Discourse Strategies*. Cambridge: Cambridge University Press.

Gumperz, John J. 1996. Introduction to part IV. In John J. Gumperz and Stephen C. Levinson (eds), *Rethinking Linguistic Relativity*. Cambridge: Cambridge University Press, 359–73.

Guy, Gregory. 1994. The phonology of variation. In Katherine Beals, Jeanette Denton, Robert Knippen, Lynette Melnar, Hisami Suzuki and Erica Zeinfeld (eds), *Papers from the 30th Regional Meeting of the Chicago Linguistic Society. Volume 2: The Parasession on Variation in Linguistic Theory*. Chicago: Chicago Linguistics Society, 133–49.

Haugen, Einar. 1966. Dialect, language, nation. *American Anthropologist* 68: 922–35.

Haugen, Einar. 1987. Language planning. In U. Ammon, N. Dittmar and J. K. Mattheier (eds), *Sociolinguistics. Soziolinguistik. An International Handbook of the Science of Language and Society. Ein internationales Handbuch zur Wissenschaft von Sprache und Gesellschaft*. Volume 1. Berlin and New York: Mouton de Gruyter, 626–37.

Hogg, Richard M. (general ed.). 1992–2001. *The Cambridge History of the English Language*. 6 volumes. Cambridge: Cambridge University Press.

Hogg, Richard M. 2002. *An Introduction to Old English.* Edinburgh: Edinburgh University Press.

Holmes, Janet. 2001. *An Introduction to Sociolinguistics.* 2nd edition. London: Pearson.

Horobin, Simon and Jeremy Smith. 2002. *An Introduction to Middle English.* Edinburgh: Edinburgh University Press.

Hudson, Richard A. 1986. Sociolinguistics and the theory of grammar. *Linguistics* 24: 1053–78

Hudson, Richard A. 1996. *Sociolinguistics.* 2nd edition. Cambridge: Cambridge University Press.

Hudson, Richard A. 1997. Inherent variability and linguistic theory. *Cognitive Linguistics* 8: 73–108.

Hudson, Richard A. 2007. *Language Networks: The New Word Grammar.* Oxford: Oxford University Press.

Humphrys, John. 2004. *Lost for Words: The Mangling and Manipulation of the English Language.* London: Hodder.

Jenkins, Jennifer. 2003. *World Englishes.* London: Routledge.

Jones, Charles. 2002. *The English Language in Scotland: An Introduction to Scots.* East Linton: Tuckwell Press.

Kachru, Braj. 1985. Standards, codification and sociolinguistic realism: The English language in the outer circle. In Randolph Quirk and Henry Widdowson (eds), *English in the World: Teaching and Learning the Language and Literatures.* Cambridge: Cambridge University Press, 11–30.

Kachru, Braj, Yamuna Kachru and Cecil L. Nelson (eds). 2006. *The Handbook of World Englishes.* Oxford: Blackwell.

Kerswill, Paul. 2002. Koineization and accommodation. In J. K. Chambers, Peter Trudgill and Natalie Schilling-Estes (eds), *The Handbook of Language Variation and Change.* Oxford: Blackwell, 669–702.

Kerswill, Paul. 2003. Dialect levelling and geographical diffusion in British English. In David Britain and Jenny Cheshire (eds), *Social Dialectology: In Honour of Peter Trudgill.* Amsterdam and Philadelphia: John Benjamins, 223–43.

Kerswill, Paul and Peter Trudgill. 2005. The birth of new dialects. In Peter Auer, Frans Hinskens and Paul Kerswill (eds), *Dialect Change: Convergence and Divergence in European Languages.* Cambridge: Cambridge University Press, 196–220.

Kerswill, Paul, Eivind Nessa Torgersen and Susan Fox. 2008. Reversing 'drift': Innovation and diffusion in the London diphthong system. *Language Variation and Change* 20: 451–91.

Kloss, Heinz. 1967. 'Abstand' languages and 'Ausbau' languages. *Anthropological Linguistics* 9: 29–41.

Kloss, Heinz. 1969. *Research Possibilities on Group Bilingualism: A Report.* Quebec: International Center for Research on Bilingualism.

Kortmann, Bernd, Kate Burridge, Raj Mesthrie, Edgar Schneider and Clive Upton. 2004. *A Handbook of Varieties of English: A Multimedia Reference Tool.* Berlin: Mouton de Gruyter.

Kroch, Anthony. 1994. Morphosyntactic variation. In Katherine Beals, Jeanette Denton, Robert Knippen, Lynette Melnar, Hisami Suzuki and Erica Zeinfeld (eds), *Papers from the 30th Regional Meeting of the Chicago Linguistic Society. Volume 2: The Parasession on Variation in Linguistic Theory.* Chicago: Chicago Linguistics Society, 180–201.

Labov, William. 1966. *The Social Stratification of English in New York City.* Washington, DC: Center for Applied Linguistics.

Labov, William. 1972. *Sociolinguistic Patterns.* Philadelphia: University of Pennsylvania Press.

Labov, William. 1989. The exact description of the speech community: Short-*a* in Philadelphia. In Ralph Fasold and Deborah Schiffrin (eds), *Language Change and Variation.* Amsterdam and Philadelphia: John Benjamins, 1–57.

Labov, William. 1990. The intersection of sex and social class in the course of linguistic change. *Language Variation and Change* 2: 205–54.

Labov, William. 1994. *Principles of Linguistic Change. Volume 1: Internal Factors.* Oxford: Blackwell.

Labov, William. 2001. *Principles of Linguistic Change. Volume 2: Social Factors.* Oxford: Blackwell.

Labov, William. 2007. Transmission and diffusion. *Language* 83: 344–87.

Labov, William, Sharon Ash and Charles Boberg. 2005. *The Atlas of North American English: Phonetics, Phonology and Sound Change.* Berlin and New York: Mouton de Gruyter.

Lass, Roger. 1999. Introduction. In Roger Lass (ed.), *The Cambridge History of the English Language. Volume III: 1476–1776.* Cambridge: Cambridge University Press, 1–12.

Lavandera, Beatrice. 1978. Where does the sociolinguistic variable stop? *Language in Society* 7: 171–82.

Lave, Jean and Etienne Wenger. 1991. *Situated Learning: Legitimate Peripheral Participation.* Cambridge: Cambridge University Press.

Le Page, Robert B. and Andrée Tabouret-Keller. 1985. *Acts of Identity: Creole-Based Approaches to Language and Ethnicity.* Cambridge: Cambridge University Press.

Llamas, Carmen. 2007. 'A place between places': Language and identities in a border town. *Language in Society* 36: 579–604.

Lo Bianco, Joseph. 2004. Language planning as applied linguistics. In Alan Davies and Catherine Elder (eds), *The Handbook of Applied Linguistics.* Oxford: Blackwell, 738–63.

Lyons, John (ed.). 1970. *New Horizons in Linguistics.* Harmondsworth: Penguin.

McArthur, Tom. 1998. *The English Languages.* Cambridge: Cambridge University Press.

McArthur, Tom. 2006. English world-wide in the twentieth century. In Lynda Mugglestone (ed.), *The Oxford History of English.* Oxford: Oxford University Press, 360–93.

McMahon, April. 1994. *Understanding Language Change.* Cambridge: Cambridge University Press.

McMahon, April. 2002. *An Introduction to English Phonology*. Edinburgh: Edinburgh University Press.

McWhorter, John H. 2003. Pidgins and creoles as models of language change: The state of the art. *Annual Review of Applied Linguistics* 23: 202–12.

Marshall, Jonathan. 2005. *Language Change and Sociolinguistics: Rethinking Social Networks*. London: Palgrave.

Mees, Inger M. and Beverley Collins. 1999. Cardiff: A real-time study of glottalisation. In Paul Foukes and Gerard J. Docherty (eds), *Urban Voices: Accent Studies in the British Isles*. London: Arnold, 185–202.

Mesthrie, Rajend, Joan Swann, Ana Deumert and William Leap. 2009. *Introducing Sociolinguistics*. 2nd edition. Edinburgh: Edinburgh University Press.

Meyerhoff, Miriam. 2002. Communities of practice. In J. K. Chambers, Peter Trudgill and Natalie Schilling-Estes (eds), *The Handbook of Language Variation and Change*. Oxford: Blackwell, 526–48.

Meyerhoff, Miriam. 2006. *Introducing Sociolinguistics*. London: Routledge.

Meyerhoff, Miriam and Nancy Niedzielski. 2003. The globalisation of vernacular variation. *Journal of Sociolinguistics* 7: 534–55.

Milroy, James. 1983. On the sociolinguistic history of /h/-dropping in English. In Michael Davenport, Erik Hansen and Hans Frede Nielsen (eds), *Current Topics in English Historical Linguistics*. Odense: Odense University Press, 37–53.

Milroy, James. 1992. *Linguistic Variation and Change: On the Historical Sociolinguistics of English*. Oxford: Blackwell.

Milroy, James and Lesley Milroy. 1998. *Authority in Language: Investigating Standard English*. 3rd edition. London: Routledge.

Milroy, Lesley. 2002. Social networks. In J. K. Chambers, Peter Trudgill and Natalie Schilling-Estes (eds), *The Handbook of Language Variation and Change*. Oxford: Blackwell, 549–72.

Milroy, Lesley and Matthew Gordon. 2003. *Sociolinguistics: Method and Interpretation*. Oxford: Blackwell.

Montgomery, Michael. 2001. British and Irish antecedents. In John Algeo (ed.), *The Cambridge History of the English Language. Volume VI: English in North America*. Cambridge: Cambridge University Press, 86–153.

Montgomery, Michael and Joseph Sargent Hall. 2004. *Dictionary of Smoky Mountain English*. Knoxville, TN: University of Tennessee Press.

Moore, Emma. 2004. Sociolinguistic style: A multidimensional resource for shared identity creation. *Canadian Journal of Linguistics* 49: 375–96.

Mufwene, Salikoko S. 2006. Pidgins and creoles. In Braj Kachru, Yamuna Kachru and Cecil L. Nelson (eds), *The Handbook of World Englishes*. Oxford: Blackwell, 313–27.

Mufwene, Salikoko S. 2008. *Language Evolution: Contact, Competition and Change*. London: Continuum.

Mugglestone, Lynda. 2003. *Talking Proper: The Rise of Accent as Social Symbol*. 2nd edition. Oxford: Oxford University Press.

Mugglestone, Lynda. 2006. English in the nineteenth century. In Lynda Mugglestone (ed.), *The Oxford History of English*. Oxford: Oxford University Press, 274–304.

Mühlhäusler, Peter. 1997. *Pidgin and Creole Linguistics*. 2nd edition. London: Westminster Press.

Myers-Scotton, Carol. 1997. *Duelling Languages: Grammatical Structure in Codeswitching*. Oxford: Oxford University Press.

Nevalainen, Terttu. 1999. Early Modern English lexis and semantics. In Roger Lass (ed.), *The Cambridge History of the English Language. Volume III: 1476–1776*. Cambridge: Cambridge University Press, 332–458.

Nevalainen, Terttu. 2006. *An Introduction to Early Modern English*. Edinburgh: Edinburgh University Press.

Nevalainen, Terttu and Helena Raumolin-Brunberg (eds). 1996. *Sociolinguistics and Language History: Studies Based on the Corpus of Early English Correspondence*. Amsterdam: Rodopi.

Nevalainen, Terttu and Helena Raumolin-Brunberg. 2003. *Historical Sociolinguistics: Language Change in Tudor and Stuart England*. London: Longman.

Nevalainen, Terttu and Ingrid Tieken-Boon van Ostade. 2006. Standardisation. In Richard Hogg and David Denison (eds), *A History of the English Language*. Cambridge: Cambridge University Press, 271–311.

Newmeyer, Frederick J. 2003. Grammar is grammar and usage is usage. *Language* 79: 682–707.

Niedzielski, Nancy and Dennis Preston. 2003. *Folk Linguistics*. 2nd edition. Berlin and New York: Mouton de Gruyter.

Oliver, Jamie. 2000. *The Return of the Naked Chef*. London: Penguin.

Omoniyi, Tope. 2006. Hip-hop through the world Englishes lens: A response to globalization. *World Englishes* 25: 195–208.

Orton, Harold, Eugene Dieth and P. M. Tilling. 1962–71. *Survey of English Dialects: Basic Materials*. Introduction and 4 volumes. Leeds: Arnold.

Patrick, Peter. 2002. The speech community. In J. K. Chambers, Peter Trudgill and Natalie Schilling Estes (eds), *The Handbook of Language Variation and Change*. Oxford: Blackwell, 573–97.

Pennycook, Alastair. 1994. *The Cultural Politics of English as an International Language*. London: Longman.

Petyt, K. M. 1980. *The Study of Dialect: An Introduction to Dialectology*. London: Deutsch.

Phillipson, Robert. 1992. *Linguistic Imperialism*. Oxford: Oxford University Press.

Phillipson, Robert. 2003. *English-Only Europe? Challenging Language Policy*. London: Routledge.

Pickering, John. 1816. *A Vocabulary, or Collection of Words which have been Supposed to be Peculiar to the United States of America*. Boston: Cummings and Hilliard.

Podesva, Robert J., Sarah J. Roberts and Kathryn Campbell-Kibler. 2002. Sharing resources and indexing meaning in the production of gay styles. In Kathryn Campbell-Kibler, Robert J. Podesva, Sarah J. Roberts and Andrew

Wong (eds), *Language and Sexuality: Contesting Meaning in Theory and Practice.* Stanford: CSLI, 175–89.

Preston, Dennis. 2002. Language with an attitude. In J. K. Chambers, Peter Trudgill and Natalie Schilling Estes (eds), *The Handbook of Language Variation and Change.* Oxford: Blackwell, 40–66.

Rampton, Ben. 1999. Crossing. *Journal of Linguistic Anthropology* 9: 54–6.

Riazi, Abdolmehdi. 2005. The four language stages in the history of Iran. In Angel Lin and Peter Martin (eds), *Decolonisation, Globalisation: Language-in-Education Policy and Practice.* Clevedon: Multilingual Matters, 100–16.

Rickford, John. 1977. The question of prior creolization in Black English. In Albert Valdman (ed.), *Pidgin and Creole Linguistics.* Bloomington: Indiana University Press, 190–221.

Rickford, John. 1986. The need for new approaches to social class analysis in sociolinguistics. *Language and Communication* 6: 215–21.

Romaine, Suzanne. 1988. *Pidgin and Creole Languages.* London: Longman.

Rowicka, Grażyna J. 2005. American Indian English: The Quinault case. *English World Wide* 26: 301–24.

Schilling-Estes, Natalie. 2002. Investigating stylistic variation. In J. K. Chambers, Peter Trudgill and Natalie Schilling-Estes (eds), *The Handbook of Language Variation and Change.* Oxford: Blackwell, 375–401.

Schneider, Edgar. 2007. *Postcolonial English: Varieties around the World.* Cambridge: Cambridge University Press.

Schreier, Daniel. 2002. Dynamic mixing or archaic retention? The ambiguous case of 'completive done' in Tristan da Cunha English. *Diachronica* 19: 135–76.

Schreier, Daniel. 2003. *Isolation and Language Change: Contemporary and Sociohistorical Evidence from Tristan da Cunha English.* Basingstoke: Palgrave Macmillan.

Sebba, Mark. 1997. *Contact Languages: Pidgins and Creoles.* London: Macmillan.

Simango, Ron. 2006. East Africa/Ostafrika. In In U. Ammon, N. Dittmar, J. K. Mattheier and P. Trudgill (eds), *Sociolinguistics. Soziolinguistik. An International Handbook of the Science of Language and Society. Ein internationales Handbuch zur Wissenschaft von Sprache und Gesellschaft.* 2nd edition. Berlin: Mouton de Gruyter, 1964–71.

Singh, Ishtla. 2000. *Pidgins and Creoles: An Introduction.* London: Arnold.

Smith, Neil. 1989. *The Twitter Machine: Reflections on Language.* Oxford: Blackwell.

Spolsky, Bernard. 2004. *Language Policy.* Cambridge: Cambridge University Press.

Stuart-Smith, Jane and Claire Timmins. 2007. Talkin' Jockney? Variation and change in Glaswegian accent. *Journal of Sociolinguistics* 11: 221–60.

Swann, Joan, Rajend Mesthrie, Ana Deumart and Theresa M. Lillis. 2004. *A Dictionary of Sociolinguistics.* Edinburgh: Edinburgh University Press.

Tagliamonte, Sali A. 2006. *Analysing Sociolinguistic Variation.* Cambridge: Cambridge University Press.

Thomason, Sarah. 2001. *Language Contact: An Introduction.* Edinburgh: Edinburgh University Press.

Tieken-Boon van Ostade, Ingrid. 2000. Normative studies in England. In Sylvain Auroux, E. F. K. Koerner, Hans-J. Niederehe and Kees Versteegh (eds), *History of the Language Sciences.* Berlin and New York: Walter de Gruyter, 876–87.

Tieken-Boon van Ostade, Ingrid. 2006. English at the onset of the normative tradition. In Lynda Mugglestone (ed.), *The Oxford History of English.* Oxford: Oxford University Press, 240–73.

Tomasello, Michael. 2003. *Constructing a Language: A Usage-Based Theory of Language Acquisition.* Cambridge, MA: Harvard University Press.

Toon, Thomas. 1983. *The Politics of Early English Sound Change.* New York and London: Academic Press.

Toon, Thomas. 1992. Old English dialectology. In Richard M. Hogg (ed.), *The Cambridge History of the English Language. Volume I: The Beginnings to 1066.* Cambridge: Cambridge University Press, 409–51.

Trudgill, Peter. 1974. *The Social Differentiation of English in Norwich.* Cambridge: Cambridge University Press.

Trudgill, Peter. 1986. *Dialects in Contact.* Oxford: Blackwell.

Trudgill, Peter. 1999a. *The Dialects of England.* 2nd edition. Oxford: Blackwell.

Trudgill, Peter. 1999b. Norwich: Endogenous and exogenous linguistic change. In Paul Foulkes and Gerard J. Docherty (eds), *Urban Voices: Accent Studies in the British Isles.* London: Arnold, 124–40.

Trudgill, Peter. 2003. *A Glossary of Sociolinguistics.* Edinburgh: Edinburgh University Press.

Trudgill, Peter. 2004. *New Dialect Formation: The Inevitability of Colonial Englishes.* Edinburgh: Edinburgh University Press.

Wales, Katie. 2006. *Northern English: A Social and Cultural History.* Cambridge: Cambridge University Press.

Wardhaugh, Ronald. 2010. *An Introduction to Sociolinguistics.* 6th edition. Oxford: Blackwell.

Watson, Kevin. 2006. Phonological resistance and innovation in the north-west of England. *English Today* 22: 55–61.

Watt, Dominic and Lesley Milroy. 1999. Variation in three Tyneside vowels: Is this dialect levelling? In Paul Foulkes and Gerry J. Docherty (eds), *Urban Voices: Accent Studies in the British Isles.* London: Arnold, 25–46.

Weinreich, Uriel, William Labov and Marvin I. Herzog. 1968. Empirical foundations for a theory of language change. In Winifred P. Lehmann and Yakov Malkiel (eds), *Directions for Historical Linguistics: A Symposium.* Austin: University of Texas Press, 95–188.

Wells, John C. 1982. *Accents of English.* 3 volumes. Cambridge: Cambridge University Press.

Wenger, Etienne. 1998. *Communities of Practice: Learning, Meaning and Identity.* Cambridge: Cambridge University Press.

Williams, Ann and Paul Kerswill. 1999. Dialect levelling: Change and continuity in Milton Keynes, Reading and Hull. In Paul Foulkes and Gerard J.

Docherty (eds), *Urban Voices: Accent Studies in the British Isles.* London: Arnold, 141–62.

Winford, Donald. 2003. *An Introduction to Contact Linguistics.* Oxford: Blackwell.

Wright, Marta. 2001. More than just chanting: Multilingual literacies, ideology and teaching methodologies in rural Eritrea. In Brian Street (ed.), *Literacy and Development: Ethnographic Perspectives.* London: Routledge, 61–77.

Index